POEMS BY
WALT WHITMAN

By

WALT WHITMAN

Selected and edited by

WILLIAM MICHAEL ROSSETTI

First published in 1868

British Library Cataloguing-in-Publication Data
A catalogue record for this book is available
from the British Library

"Or si sa il nome, o per tristo o per buono,
E si sa pure al mondo ch'io ci sono."

— MICHELANGELO.

"That Angels are human forms, or men, I have seen a
thousand times. I have also frequently told them that
men in the Christian world are in such gross ignorance
respecting Angels and Spirits as to suppose them to be
minds without a form, or mere thoughts, of which they
have no other idea than as something ethereal possessing
a vital principle. To the first or ultimate heaven also
correspond the forms of man's body, called its members,
organs, and viscera. Thus the corporeal part of man is that
in which heaven ultimately closes, and upon which, as on
its base, it rests."

— SWEDENBORG.

"Yes, truly, it is a great thing for a nation that it get an
articulate voice—that it produce a man who will speak
forth melodiously what the heart of it means."

— CARLYLE.

"Les efforts de vos ennemis contre vous, leurs cris, leur
rage impuissante, et leurs petits succès, ne doivent pas vous
effrayer; ce ne sont que des égratignures sur les épaules
d'Hercule."

— ROBESPIERRE.

TO WILLIAM BELL SCOTT.

———————————

DEAR SCOTT,

Among various gifts which I have received from you, tangible and intangible, was a copy of the original quarto edition of Whitman's *Leaves of Grass*, which you presented to me soon after its first appearance in 1855. At a time when few people on this side of the Atlantic had looked into the book, and still fewer had found in it anything save matter for ridicule, you had appraised it, and seen that its value was real and great. A true poet and a strong thinker like yourself was indeed likely to see that. I read the book eagerly, and perceived that its substantiality and power were still ahead of any eulogium with which it might have come commended to me—and, in fact, ahead of most attempts that could be made at verbal definition of them.

Some years afterwards, getting to know our friend Swinburne, I found with much satisfaction that he also was an ardent (not of course a *blind*) admirer of Whitman. Satisfaction, and a degree almost of surprise; for his intense sense of poetic refinement of form in his own works and his exacting acuteness as a critic might have seemed likely to carry him away from Whitman in sympathy at least, if not in actual latitude of perception. Those who find the American poet "utterly formless," "intolerably rough and floundering," "destitute of the A B C of art," and the like, might not unprofitably ponder this very different estimate of him by the author of *Atalanta in Calydon*.

May we hope that now, twelve years after the first appearance of *Leaves of Grass,* the English reading public may be prepared for a selection of Whitman's poems, and soon hereafter for a complete edition of them? I trust this may prove to be the case.

At any rate, it has been a great gratification to me to be concerned in the experiment; and this is enhanced by my being enabled to associate with it your name, as that of an early and well-qualified appreciator of Whitman, and no less as that of a dear friend.

Yours affectionately,

W. M. ROSSETTI.

October 1867.

CONTENTS

Walt Whitman

Leaves of Grass.

Songs of Parting.

WALT WHITMAN

Walt Whitman was born on 31st May 1819 in the Town of Huntington, Long Island, New York, USA. He was the second of nine children of Walter Whitman and Louisa Van Velsor Whitman. In part due to a series of bad investments, the family lived in various homes in the Brooklyn area, and Whitman recalled his childhood as generally restless and unhappy, given his family's difficult economic status. Whitman finished his formal schooling at age eleven, and immediately sought employment to aid his family. He worked in an office of a legal firm and later as an apprentice and printer's devil for the weekly Long Island newspaper, the *Patriot*. The following summer, Whitman took a job with the leading Whig newspaper the *Long-Island Star*, and it was here that he developed a strong interest in reading, writing and theatre. He also anonymously published some of his earliest poetry in the *New York Mirror*.

After a brief sojourn as a teacher, living back with his family in Long Island, Whitman returned to New York to establish his own newspaper; the *Long Islander*. He embarked on this project in the spring of 1838, but sold the paper to E.O. Crowell after only ten months. From 1840-41 Whitman attempted to further his career in teaching, but with little success, he returned to writing. During this time, Whitman published a series of ten editorials, called *Sun-Down Papers—From the Desk of a Schoolmaster*, in three newspapers between the winter of 1840 and July 1841. In these essays, he adopted a constructed persona, a technique he would employ throughout his career. It was not until 1850 that Whitman began writing what would later become *Leaves of Grass;* a collection of poetry which he continued editing and revising until his death. The first edition was a success, and stirred up significant interest, partly due to the praise it received by Ralph Waldo Emerson. However the volume, which Whitman intended as 'a distinctly American epic', attracted substantial criticism for its 'offensive' and 'crude' sexual themes. It deviated from the historic use of an elevated hero and instead assumed the identity of the common person; part of the transition in American literature, moving away from transcendentalism towards realism. In light of the contemporary criticism, Whitman's sexuality is often discussed alongside his poetry. Though biographers continue to debate his sexuality, he is usually described as either homosexual or bisexual - yet this remains speculation.

Whitman lived through the American Civil war, and volunteered as a nurse in army hospital, later serving as a clerk in the *Bureau of Indian Affairs* in the Department of the Interior. In June of 1865, Whitman was fired from his job – most likely on moral grounds, by the former Iowa Senator James Harlan, after he found an 1860 edition of *Leaves of Grass.* Whitman's friend William Douglas O'Connor, a well-connected poet and newspaper editor was incensed by this iniquitousness, and wrote a pamphlet defending Whitman as a wholesome patriot, greatly increasing his popularity. Further adding to Whitman's fame during this period was the publication of *O Captain! My Captain!;* a relatively conventional poem chronicling the death of Abraham Lincoln. It was the only poem to appear in anthologies during Whitman's lifetime. The author then moved onto work at the Attorney General's office, interviewing former Confederate soldiers for Presidential Pardons - an occupation which was more to Whitman's taste. He later wrote to a friend; 'there are real characters among them... and you know I have a fancy for anything out of the ordinary.' During this time, Whitman succeeded in finding a publisher for *Leaves of Grass* (eventually issued in 1871), the same year it was mistakenly reported that its author died in a railroad accident. Only two years after this great personal success, Whitman suffered a paralytic stroke (early in 1873) and was induced to move to the home of his brother in

New Jersey. Whilst there, he was very productive, publishing three versions of *Leaves of Grass*, as well as other works. This was also the last point at which Whitman was fully mobile, and he received many famous authors, including Oscar Wilde and Thomas Eakins. In 1884, he bought his own house, remaining in New Jersey, but became completely bedridden soon after. In the last week of his life, Whitman was too weak even to lift a knife or fork, and wrote; 'I suffer all the time: I have no relief, no escape: it is monotony—monotony—monotony—in pain.' He died from diminished lung capacity, the result of bronchial pneumonia and an abscess on the chest, on 26 March 1892.

By the time of his death, Whitman had become a veritable national celebrity, and a public viewing of his body was held at his home; an event which attracted over one thousand people in three hours. His coffin was barely visible because of all the flowers and wreaths. Whitman was buried four days later at Harleigh Cemetery in Camden, New Jersey. He has since been eulogised as America's first 'poet of democracy', due to his uncanny ability to write in the American character, and remains an enduring and much loved literary figure to this day.

PREFATORY NOTICE.

During the summer of 1867 I had the opportunity (which I had often wished for) of expressing in print my estimate and admiration of the works of the American poet Walt Whitman. [1] Like a stone dropped into a pond, an article of that sort may spread out its concentric circles of consequences. One of these is the invitation which I have received to edit a selection from Whitman's writings; virtually the first sample of his work ever published in England, and offering the first tolerably fair chance he has had of making his way with English readers on his own showing. Hitherto, such readers—except the small percentage of them to whom it has happened to come across the poems in some one of their American editions—have picked acquaintance with them only through the medium of newspaper extracts and criticisms, mostly short-sighted, sneering, and depreciatory, and rather intercepting than forwarding the candid construction which people might be willing to put upon the poems, alike in their beauties and their aberrations. Some English critics, no doubt, have been more discerning—as W. J. Fox, of old, in the *Dispatch*, the writer of the notice in the *Leader*, and of late two in the *Pall Mall Gazette* and the *London Review*;[2] but these have been the exceptions among us, the great majority of the reviewers presenting that happy and familiar critical combination—scurrility and superciliousness.

As it was my lot to set down so recently several of the considerations which seem to me most essential and most obvious in regard to Whitman's writings, I can scarcely now recur to the subject without either repeating something of what I then said, or else leaving unstated some points of principal importance. I shall therefore adopt the simplest course—that

17

of summarising the critical remarks in my former article; after which, I shall leave without further development (ample as is the amount of development most of them would claim) the particular topics there glanced at, and shall proceed to some other phases of the subject.

Whitman republished in 1867 his complete poetical works in one moderate- sized volume, consisting of the whole *Leaves of Grass*, with a sort of supplement thereto named *Songs before Parting*,[3] and of the *Drum Taps*, with its *Sequel*. It has been intimated that he does not expect to write any more poems, unless it might be in expression of the religious side of man's nature. However, one poem on the last American harvest sown and reaped by those who had been soldiers in the great war, has already appeared since the volume in question, and has been republished in England.

Whitman's poems present no trace of rhyme, save in a couple or so of chance instances. Parts of them, indeed, may be regarded as a warp of prose amid the weft of poetry, such as Shakespeare furnishes the precedent for in drama. Still there is a very powerful and majestic rhythmical sense throughout.

Lavish and persistent has been the abuse poured forth upon Whitman by his own countrymen; the tricklings of the British press give but a moderate idea of it. The poet is known to repay scorn with scorn. Emerson can, however, from the first be claimed as on Whitman's side; nor, it is understood after some inquiry, has that great thinker since then retreated from this position in fundamentals, although his admiration may have entailed some worry upon him, and reports of his recantation have been rife. Of other writers on Whitman's side, expressing themselves with no measured enthusiasm, one may cite Mr. M. D. Conway; Mr. W. D. O'Connor, who wrote a pamphlet named *The Good Grey Poet*; and Mr. John Burroughs, author of *Walt Whitman as Poet and Person*, published quite recently in New York. His thorough-paced admirers declare Whitman to be beyond rivalry *the* poet of the epoch; an estimate which, startling as it will sound at the first, may nevertheless be upheld, on the grounds that Whitman is beyond all his competitors a man of the period, one of audacious personal ascendant, incapable of all compromise, and an initiator in the scheme and form of his works.

Certain faults are charged against him, and, as far as they are true, shall frankly stand confessed—some of them as very serious faults. Firstly, he speaks on occasion of gross things in gross, crude, and plain terms. Secondly, he uses some words absurd or ill-constructed, others which produce a jarring effect in poetry, or indeed in any lofty literature. Thirdly, he sins from time to time by being obscure, fragmentary, and agglomerative—giving long strings of successive and detached items, not, however, devoid of a certain primitive effectiveness. Fourthly, his self-assertion is boundless; yet not always to be understood as strictly or merely personal to himself, but sometimes as vicarious, the poet speaking on behalf of all men, and every man and woman. These and any other faults appear most harshly on a cursory reading; Whitman is a poet who bears and needs to be read as a whole, and then the volume and torrent of his power carry the disfigurements along with it, and away.

The subject-matter of Whitman's poems, taken individually, is absolutely miscellaneous: he touches upon any and every subject. But he has prefixed to his last edition an "Inscription" in the following terms, showing that the key-words of the whole book are two—"One's-self" and "En Masse:"—

> Small is the theme of the following chant, yet the
> greatest.—namely, ONE'S-SELF; that wondrous thing,
> a simple separate person. That, for the use of the New
> World, I sing.
> Man's physiology complete, from top to toe, I sing. Not
> physiognomy alone, nor brain alone, is worthy for
> the Muse: I say the form complete is worthier far. The
> female equally with the male I sing.

19

Nor cease at the theme of One's-self. I speak the word of
the modern, the word EN MASSE.
My days I sing, and the lands—with interstice I knew of
hapless war.
O friend, whoe'er you are, at last arriving hither to
commence, I feel through every leaf the pressure
of your hand, which I return. And thus upon our
journey linked together let us go.

The book, then, taken as a whole, is the poem both of
Personality and of Democracy; and, it may be added, of
American nationalism. It is *par excellence* the modern poem.
It is distinguished also by this peculiarity— that in it the most
literal view of things is continually merging into the most
rhapsodic or passionately abstract. Picturesqueness it has, but
mostly of a somewhat patriarchal kind, not deriving from the
"word-painting" of the *littérateur*; a certain echo of the old
Hebrew poetry may even be caught in it, extra-modern though
it is. Another most prominent and pervading quality of the
book is the exuberant physique of the author. The conceptions
are throughout those of a man in robust health, and might alter
much under different conditions.

Further, there is a strong tone of paradox in Whitman's
writings. He is both a realist and an optimist in extreme measure:
he contemplates evil as in some sense not existing, or, if existing,
then as being of as much importance as anything else. Not that he
is a materialist; on the contrary, he is a most strenuous assertor of
the soul, and, with the soul, of the body as its infallible associate
and vehicle in the present frame of things. Neither does he drift
into fatalism or indifferentism; the energy of his temperament,
and ever-fresh sympathy with national and other developments,
being an effectual bar to this. The paradoxical element of the
poems is such that one may sometimes find them in conflict with
what has preceded, and would not be much surprised if they
said at any moment the reverse of whatever they do say. This is

mainly due to the multiplicity of the aspects of things, and to the immense width of relation in which Whitman stands to all sorts and all aspects of them.

But the greatest of this poet's distinctions is his absolute and entire originality. He may be termed formless by those who, not without much reason to show for themselves, are wedded to the established forms and ratified refinements of poetic art; but it seems reasonable to enlarge the canon till it includes so great and startling a genius, rather than to draw it close and exclude him. His work is practically certain to stand as archetypal for many future poetic efforts—so great is his power as an originator, so fervid his initiative. It forms incomparably the *largest* performance of our period in poetry. Victor Hugo's *Légende des Siècles* alone might be named with it for largeness, and even that with much less of a new starting-point in conception and treatment. Whitman breaks with all precedent. To what he himself perceives and knows he has a personal relation of the intensest kind: to anything in the way of prescription, no relation at all. But he is saved from isolation by the depth of his Americanism; with the movement of his predominant nation he is moved. His comprehension, energy, and tenderness are all extreme, and all inspired by actualities. And, as for poetic genius, those who, without being ready to concede that faculty to Whitman, confess his iconoclastic boldness and his Titanic power of temperament, working in the sphere of poetry, do in effect confess his genius as well.

Such, still further condensed, was the critical summary which I gave of Whitman's position among poets. It remains to say something a little more precise of the particular qualities of his works. And first, not to slur over defects, I shall extract some sentences from a letter which a friend, most highly entitled to form and express an opinion on any poetic question—one, too, who abundantly upholds the greatness of Whitman as a poet—has addressed to me with regard to the criticism above condensed. His observations, though severe on this individual point, appear to me not other than correct. "I don't think that you quite put strength enough into your blame on one side, while you make at least enough of minor faults or eccentricities. To me it seems always that Whitman's great flaw is a fault of debility, not an excess of strength—I mean his bluster. His own personal and national self-reliance and arrogance, I need not tell you, I applaud, and sympathise and rejoice in; but the blatant ebullience of feeling and speech, at times, is feeble for so great a poet of so great a people. He is in part certainly the poet of democracy; but not wholly, *because* he tries so openly to be, and asserts so violently that he is— always as if he was fighting the case out on a platform. This is the only thing I really or greatly dislike or revolt from. On the whole" (adds my correspondent), "my admiration and enjoyment of his greatness grow keener and warmer every time I think of him"—a feeling, I may be permitted to observe, which is fully shared by myself, and, I suppose, by all who consent in any adequate measure to recognise Whitman, and to yield themselves to his influence.

To continue. Besides originality and daring, which have been already insisted upon, width and intensity are leading characteristics of his writings—width both of subject-matter and of comprehension, intensity of self-absorption into what the poet contemplates and expresses. He scans and presents an enormous panorama, unrolled before him as from a mountain-top; and yet, whatever most large or most minute or casual thing his eye glances upon, that he enters into with a depth of affection which identifies him with it for a time, be the object what it may. There is a singular interchange also of actuality and of ideal substratum and suggestion. While he sees men, with even abnormal exactness and sympathy, as men, he sees them also "as trees walking," and admits us to perceive that the whole show is in a measure spectral and unsubstantial, and the mask of a larger and profounder reality beneath it, of which it is giving perpetual intimations and auguries. He is the poet indeed of literality, but of passionate and significant literality, full of indirections as well as directness, and of readings between the lines. If he is the 'cutest of Yankees, he is also as truly an enthusiast as any the most typical poet. All his faculties and performance glow into a white heat of brotherliness; and there is a *poignancy* both of tenderness and of beauty about his finer works which discriminates them quite as much as their modernness, audacity, or any other exceptional point. If the reader wishes to see the great and more intimate powers of Whitman in their fullest expression, he may consult the *Nocturn for the Death of Lincoln*; than which it would be difficult to find anywhere a purer, more elevated, more poetic, more ideally abstract, or at the same time more pathetically personal, threnody—uniting the thrilling chords of grief, of beauty, of triumph, and of final unfathomed satisfaction. With all his singularities, Whitman is a master of words and of sounds: he has them at his command—made for, and instinct with, his purpose—messengers of unsurpassable sympathy and intelligence between himself and his readers. The entire book may be called the paean of the natural man—not of the merely physical, still less of the disjunctively intellectual or spiritual man, but of him who, being a man first and foremost, is therein also a spirit and an intellect.

There is a singular and impressive intuition or revelation of Swedenborg's: that the whole of heaven is in the form of one man, and the separate societies of heaven in the forms of the several parts of man. In a large sense, the general drift of Whitman's writings, even down to the passages which read as most bluntly physical, bear a striking correspondence or analogy to this dogma. He takes man, and every organism and faculty of man, as the unit—the datum—from which all that we know, discern, and speculate, of abstract and supersensual, as well as of concrete and sensual, has to be computed. He knows of nothing nobler than that unit man; but, knowing that, he can use it for any multiple, and for any dynamical extension or recast.

Let us next obtain some idea of what this most remarkable poet—the founder of *American* poetry rightly to be so called, and the most sonorous poetic voice of the tangibilities of actual and prospective democracy—is in his proper life and person.

Walt Whitman was born at the farm-village of West Hills, Long Island, in the State of New York, and about thirty miles distant from the capital, on the 31st of May 1819. His father's family, English by origin, had already been settled in this locality for five generations. His mother, named Louisa van Velsor, was of Dutch extraction, and came from Cold Spring, Queen's County, about three miles from West Hills. "A fine-looking old lady" she has been termed in her advanced age. A large family ensued from the marriage. The father was a farmer, and afterwards a carpenter and builder; both parents adhered in religion to "the great Quaker iconoclast, Elias Hicks." Walt was schooled at Brooklyn, a suburb of New York, and began life at the age of thirteen, working as a printer, later on as a country teacher, and then as a miscellaneous press-writer in New York. From 1837 to 1848 he had, as Mr. Burroughs too promiscuously expresses it, "sounded all experiences of life, with all their passions, pleasures, and abandonments." In 1849 he began travelling, and became at New Orleans a newspaper editor, and at Brooklyn, two years afterwards, a printer. He next followed his father's business of carpenter and builder. In 1862, after the breaking-out of the great Civil War, in which his enthusiastic unionism and also his anti-slavery feelings attached him inseparably though not rancorously to the good cause of the North, he undertook the nursing of the sick and wounded in the field, writing also a correspondence in the *New York Times*. I am informed that it was through Emerson's intervention that he obtained the sanction of President Lincoln for this purpose of charity, with authority to draw the ordinary army rations; Whitman stipulating at the same time that he would not receive any remuneration for his services. The first immediate occasion of his going down to camp was on behalf of his brother, Lieutenant-Colonel George W. Whitman, of the 51st New York Veterans, who had been struck in the face by a piece of shell at Fredericksburg. From the spring of 1863 this nursing, both in the field and more especially in hospital at Washington, became his "one daily and nightly occupation;" and the strongest testimony is borne to his measureless self-devotion and kindliness in the work, and to the unbounded fascination, a kind of magnetic attraction and ascendency, which he exercised over the patients, often with the happiest sanitary results. Northerner or Southerner, the belligerents received the same tending from him. It is said that by the end of the war he had personally ministered to upwards of 100,000 sick and wounded. In a Washington hospital he caught, in the summer of 1864, the first illness he had ever known, caused by poison absorbed into the system in attending some of the worst cases of gangrene. It disabled him for six months. He returned to the hospitals towards the beginning of 1865, and obtained also a clerkship in the Department of the Interior. It should be added that, though he never actually joined the army as a combatant, he made a point of putting down his name on the enrolment- lists for the draft, to take his chance as it might happen for serving the country in arms. The reward of his devotedness came at the end of June 1865, in the form of dismissal from his clerkship by the minister, Mr. Harlan, who learned that Whitman was the author of the *Leaves of Grass*; a book whose outspokenness, or (as the official chief considered it) immorality, raised a holy horror in the ministerial breast. The poet, however, soon obtained another modest but creditable post in the office of the Attorney-General. He still visits the hospitals on Sundays, and often on other days as well.

The portrait of Mr. Whitman reproduced in the present volume is taken from an engraving after a daguerreotype given in the original *Leaves of Grass*. He is much above the average size, and noticeably well-proportioned—a model of physique and of health, and, by natural consequence, as fully and finely related to all physical facts by his bodily constitution as to all mental and spiritual facts by his mind and his consciousness. He is now, however, old-looking for his years, and might even (according to the statement of one of his enthusiasts, Mr. O'Connor) have passed for being beyond the age for the draft when the war was going on. The same gentleman, in confutation of any inferences which might be drawn from the *Leaves of Grass* by a Harlan or other Holy Willie, affirms that "one more irreproachable in his relations to the other sex lives not upon this earth"—an assertion which one must take as one finds it, having neither confirmatory nor traversing evidence at hand. Whitman has light blue eyes, a florid complexion, a fleecy beard now grey, and a quite peculiar sort of magnetism about him in relation to those with whom he comes in contact. His ordinary appearance is masculine and cheerful: he never shows depression of spirits, and is sufficiently undemonstrative, and even somewhat silent in company. He has always been carried by predilection towards the society of the common people; but is not the less for that open to refined and artistic impressions—fond of operatic and other good music, and discerning in works of art. As to either praise or blame of what he writes, he is totally indifferent, not to say scornful—having in fact a very decisive opinion of his own concerning its calibre and destinies. Thoreau, a very congenial spirit, said of Whitman, "He is Democracy;" and again, "After all, he suggests something a little more than human." Lincoln broke out into the exclamation, "Well, *he* looks like a man!" Whitman responded to the instinctive appreciation of the President, considering him (it is said by Mr. Burroughs) "by far the noblest and purest of the political characters of the time;" and, if anything can cast, in the eyes of posterity, an added halo of brightness round the unsullied personal qualities and the great doings of Lincoln, it will assuredly be the written monument reared to him by Whitman.

The best sketch that I know of Whitman as an accessible human individual is that given by Mr. Conway.[4] I borrow from it the following few details. "Having occasion to visit New York soon after the appearance of Walt Whitman's book, I was urged by some friends to search him out…. The day was excessively hot, the thermometer at nearly 100°, and the sun blazed down as only on sandy Long Island can the sun blaze.... I saw stretched upon his back, and gazing up straight at the terrible sun, the man I was seeking. With his grey clothing, his blue-grey shirt, his iron-grey hair, his swart sunburnt face and bare neck, he lay upon the brown-and-white grass—for the sun had burnt away its greenness—and was so like the earth upon which he rested that he seemed almost enough a part of it for one to pass by without recognition. I approached him, gave my name and reason for searching him out, and asked him if he did not find the sun rather hot. 'Not at all too hot,' was his reply; and he confided to me that this was one of his favourite places and attitudes for composing 'poems.' He then walked with me to his home, and took me along its narrow ways to his room. A small room of about fifteen feet square, with a single window looking out on the barren solitudes of the island; a small cot; a wash-stand with a little looking-glass hung over it from a tack in the wall; a pine table with pen, ink, and paper on it; an old line-engraving representing Bacchus, hung on the wall, and opposite a similar one of Silenus: these constituted the visible environments of Walt Whitman. There was not, apparently, a single book in the room.... The books he seemed to know and love best were the Bible, Homer, and Shakespeare: these he owned, and probably had in his pockets while we were talking. He had two studies where he read; one was the top of an omnibus, and the other a small mass of sand, then entirely uninhabited, far out in the ocean, called Coney Island.... The only distinguished contemporary he had ever met was the Rev. Henry Ward Beecher, of Brooklyn, who had visited him.... He confessed to having no talent for industry, and that his forte was 'loafing and writing poems:' he was poor, but had discovered that he could, on the whole, live magnificently on bread and water.... On no occasion did he laugh, nor indeed did I ever see him smile."

The first trace of Whitman as a writer is in the pages of the *Democratic Review* in or about 1841. Here he wrote some prose tales and sketches—poor stuff mostly, so far as I have seen of them, yet not to be wholly confounded with the commonplace. One of them is a tragic school-incident, which may be surmised to have fallen under his personal observation in his early experience as a teacher. His first poem of any sort was named *Blood Money*, in denunciation of the Fugitive Slave Law, which severed him from the Democratic party. His first considerable work was the *Leaves of Grass*. He began it in 1853, and it underwent two or three complete rewritings prior to its publication at Brooklyn in 1855, in a quarto volume—peculiar-looking, but with something perceptibly artistic about it. The type of that edition was set up entirely by himself. He was moved to undertake this formidable poetic work (as indicated in a private letter of Whitman's, from which Mr. Conway has given a sentence or two) by his sense of the great materials which America could offer for a really American poetry, and by his contempt for the current work of his compatriots—"either the poetry of an elegantly weak sentimentalism, at bottom nothing but maudlin puerilities or more or less musical verbiage, arising out of a life of depression and enervation as their result; or else that class of poetry, plays, &c., of which the foundation is feudalism, with its ideas of lords and ladies, its imported standard of gentility, and the manners of European high-life-below-stairs in every line and verse." Thus incited to poetic self-expression, Whitman (adds Mr. Conway) "wrote on a sheet of paper, in large letters, these words, 'Make the Work,' and fixed it above his table, where he could always see it whilst writing. Thenceforth every cloud that flitted over him, every distant sail, every face and form encountered, wrote a line in his book."

The *Leaves of Grass* excited no sort of notice until a letter from Emerson[5] appeared, expressing a deep sense of its power and magnitude. He termed it "the most extraordinary piece of wit and wisdom that America has yet contributed."

The edition of about a thousand copies sold off in less than a year. Towards the end of 1856 a second edition in 16mo appeared, printed in New York, also of about a thousand copies. Its chief feature was an additional poem beginning "A Woman waits for me." It excited a considerable storm. Another edition, of about four to five thousand copies, duodecimo, came out at Boston in 1860-61, including a number of new pieces. The *Drum Taps*, consequent upon the war, with their *Sequel*, which comprises the poem on Lincoln, followed in 1865; and in 1867, as I have already noted, a complete edition of all the poems, including a supplement named *Songs before Parting*. The first of all the *Leaves of Grass*, in point of date, was the long and powerful composition entitled *Walt Whitman*—perhaps the most typical and memorable of all of his productions, but shut out from the present selection for reasons given further on. The final edition shows numerous and considerable variations from all its precursors; evidencing once again that Whitman is by no means the rough-and-ready writer, panoplied in rude art and egotistic self-sufficiency, that many people suppose him to be. Even since this issue, the book has been slightly revised by its author's own hand, with a special view to possible English circulation. The copy so revised has reached me (through the liberal and friendly hands of Mr. Conway) after my selection had already been decided on; and the few departures from the last printed text which might on comparison be found in the present volume are due to my having had the advantage of following this revised copy. In all other respects I have felt bound to reproduce the last edition, without so much as considering whether here and there I might personally prefer the readings of the earlier issues.

The selection here offered to the English reader contains a little less than half the entire bulk of Whitman's poetry. My choice has proceeded upon two simple rules: first, to omit entirely every poem which could with any tolerable fairness be deemed offensive to the feelings of morals or propriety in this peculiarly nervous age; and, second, to include every remaining poem which appeared to me of conspicuous beauty or interest. I have also inserted the very remarkable prose preface which Whitman printed in the original edition of *Leaves of Grass*, an edition that has become a literary rarity. This preface has not been reproduced in any later publication, although its materials have to some extent been worked up into poems of a subsequent date.[6] From this prose composition, contrary to what has been my rule with any of the poems, it has appeared to me permissible to omit two or three short phrases which would have shocked ordinary readers, and the retention of which, had I held it obligatory, would have entailed the exclusion of the preface itself as a whole.

A few words must be added as to the indecencies scattered through Whitman's writings. Indecencies or improprieties—or, still better, deforming crudities—they may rightly be termed; to call them immoralities would be going too far. Whitman finds himself, and other men and women, to be a compound of soul and body; he finds that body plays an extremely prominent and determining part in whatever he and other mundane dwellers have cognisance of; he perceives this to be the necessary condition of things, and therefore, as he fully and openly accepts it, the right condition; and he knows of no reason why what is universally seen and known, necessary and right, should not also be allowed and proclaimed in speech. That such a view of the matter is entitled to a great deal of weight, and at any rate to candid consideration and construction, appears to me not to admit of a doubt: neither is it dubious that the contrary view, the only view which a mealy-mouthed British nineteenth century admits as endurable, amounts to the condemnation of nearly every great or eminent literary work of past time, whatever the century it belongs to, the country it comes from, the department of writing it illustrates, or the degree or sort of merit it possesses. Tenth, second, or first century before Christ—first, eighth, fourteenth, fifteenth, sixteenth, seventeenth, or even eighteenth century A.D.—it is still the same: no book whose subject-matter admits as possible of an impropriety according to current notions can be depended upon to fail of containing such impropriety,— can, if those notions are accepted as the canon, be placed with a sense of security in the hands of girls and youths, or read aloud to women; and this holds good just as much of severely moral or plainly descriptive as of avowedly playful, knowing, or licentious books. For my part, I am far from thinking that earlier state of literature, and the public feeling from which it sprang, the wrong ones— and our present condition the only right one. Equally far, therefore, am I from indignantly condemning Whitman for every startling allusion or expression which he has admitted into his book, and which I, from motives of policy, have excluded from this selection; except, indeed, that I think many of his tabooed passages are extremely raw and ugly on the ground of poetic or literary art, whatever aspect they may bear in morals. I have been rigid in exclusion, because it appears to me highly desirable that a fair verdict on Whitman should now be pronounced in England on poetic grounds alone; and because it was clearly impossible that the book, with its audacities of topic and of expression included, should run the same chance of justice, and of circulation through refined minds and hands, which may possibly be accorded to it after the rejection of all such peccant poems. As already intimated, I have not in a single instance excised any *parts* of poems: to do so would have been, I conceive, no less wrongful towards the illustrious American than repugnant, and indeed unendurable, to myself, who aspire to no Bowdlerian honours. The consequence is, that the reader loses *in toto* several important poems, and some extremely fine ones—notably the one previously alluded to, of quite exceptional value and excellence, entitled *Walt Whitman*. I sacrifice them grudgingly; and yet willingly, because I believe this to be the only thing to do with due regard to the one reasonable object which a selection can subserve—that of paving the way towards the issue and unprejudiced reception of a complete edition of the poems in England. For the benefit of misconstructionists, let me add in distinct terms that, in respect of morals and propriety, I neither admire nor approve the incriminated passages in Whitman's poems, but, on the contrary, consider that most of them would be much better away; and, in respect of art, I doubt whether even one of them deserves to be retained in the exact phraseology it at present exhibits. This, however, does not amount to saying that Whitman is a vile man, or a corrupt or corrupting writer; he is none of these.

The only division of his poems into sections, made by Whitman himself, has been noted above: *Leaves of Grass, Songs before Parting,* supplementary to the preceding, and *Drum Taps,* with their *Sequel.* The peculiar title, *Leaves of Grass,* has become almost inseparable from the name of Whitman; it seems to express with some aptness the simplicity, universality, and spontaneity of the poems to which it is applied. *Songs before Parting* may indicate that these compositions close Whitman's poetic roll. *Drum Taps* are, of course, songs of the Civil War, and their *Sequel* is mainly on the same theme: the chief poem in this last section being the one on the death of Lincoln. These titles all apply to fully arranged series of compositions. The present volume is not in the same sense a fully arranged series, but a selection: and the relation of the poems *inter se* appears to me to depend on altered conditions, which, however narrowed they are, it may be as well frankly to recognise in practice. I have therefore redistributed the poems (a latitude of action which I trust the author may not object to), bringing together those whose subject-matter seems to warrant it, however far separated they may possibly be in the original volume. At the same time, I have retained some characteristic terms used by Whitman himself, and have named my sections respectively—

1. Chants Democratic (poems of democracy).
2. Drum Taps (war songs).
3. Walt Whitman (personal poems).
4. Leaves of Grass (unclassified poems).
5. Songs of Parting (missives).

The first three designations explain themselves. The fourth,

Leaves of Grass, is not so specially applicable to the particular poems of that section here as I should have liked it to be; but I could not consent to drop this typical name. The *Songs of Parting*, my fifth section, are compositions in which the poet expresses his own sentiment regarding his works, in which he forecasts their future, or consigns them to the reader's consideration. It deserves mention that, in the copy of Whitman's last American edition revised by his own hand, as previously noticed, the series termed *Songs of Parting* has been recast, and made to consist of poems of the same character as those included in my section No. 5.

Comparatively few of Whitman's poems have been endowed by himself with titles properly so called. Most of them are merely headed with the opening words of the poems themselves—as "I was looking a long while;" "To get betimes in Boston Town;" "When lilacs last in the door-yard bloomed;" and so on. It seems to me that in a selection such a lengthy and circuitous method of identifying the poems is not desirable: I should wish them to be remembered by brief, repeatable, and significant titles. I have therefore supplied titles of my own to such pieces as bear none in the original edition: wherever a real title appears in that edition, I have retained it.

With these remarks I commend to the English reader the ensuing selection from a writer whom I sincerely believe to be, whatever his faults, of the order of *great* poets, and by no means of pretty good ones. I would urge the reader not to ask himself, and not to return any answer to the questions, whether or not this poet is like other poets—whether or not the particular application of rules of art which is found to hold good in the works of those others, and to constitute a part of their excellence, can be traced also in Whitman. Let the questions rather be—Is he powerful? Is he American? Is he new? Is he rousing? Does he feel and make me feel? I entertain no doubt as to the response which in due course of time will be returned to these questions and such as these, in America, in England, and elsewhere—or to the further question, "Is Whitman then indeed a true and a great poet?" Lincoln's verdict bespeaks the ultimate decision upon him, in his books as in his habit as he lives—"Well, *he* looks like a man."

Walt Whitman occupies at the present moment a unique position on the globe, and one which, even in past time, can have been occupied by only an infinitesimally small number of men. He is the one man who entertains and professes respecting himself the grave conviction that he is the actual and prospective founder of a new poetic literature, and a great one—a literature proportional to the material vastness and the unmeasured destinies of America: he believes that the Columbus of the continent or the Washington of the States was not more truly than himself in the future a founder and upbuilder of this America. Surely a sublime conviction, and expressed more than once in magnificent words—none more so than the lines beginning

"Come, I will make this continent indissoluble."[7]

Were the idea untrue, it would still be a glorious dream, which a man of genius might be content to live in and die for: but is it untrue? Is it not, on the contrary, true, if not absolutely, yet with a most genuine and substantial approximation? I believe it *is* thus true. I believe that Whitman is one of the huge, as yet mainly unrecognised, forces of our time; privileged to evoke, in a country hitherto still asking for its poet, a fresh, athletic, and American poetry, and predestined to be traced up to by generation after generation of believing and ardent—let us hope not servile—disciples.

"Poets are the unacknowledged legislators of the world."

Shelley, who knew what he was talking about when poetry was the subject, has said it, and with a profundity of truth Whitman seems in a peculiar degree marked out for "legislation" of the kind referred to. His voice will one day be potential or magisterial wherever the English language is spoken—that is to say, in the four corners of the earth; and in his own American hemisphere, the uttermost avatars of democracy will confess him not more their announcer than their inspirer.

W. M. ROSSETTI.
1868.

N.B.—The above prefatory notice was written in 1868, and is reproduced practically unaltered. Were it to be brought up to the present date, 1886, I should have to mention Whitman's books *Two Rivulets* and *Specimen-days and Collect*, and the fact that for several years past he has been partially disabled by a paralytic attack. He now lives at Camden, New Jersey.

W. M. R.
1886.

FOOTNOTES:

1. *See The Chronicle for 6th July 1867, article Walt Whitman's Poems.*
2. *Since this Prefatory Notice was written [in 1868], another eulogistic review of Whitman has appeared—that by Mr. Robert Buchanan, in the Broadway.*
3. *In a copy of the book revised by Whitman himself, which we have seen, this title is modified into Songs of Parting.*
4. *In the Fortnightly Review, 15th October 1866.*
5. *Mr. Burroughs (to whom I have recourse for most biographical facts concerning Whitman) is careful to note, in order that no misapprehension may arise on the subject, that, up to the time of his publishing the Leaves of Grass, the author had not read either*

the essays or the poems of Emerson.

6. *Compare, for instance, the Preface, pp. 38, 39, with the poem To a Foiled Revolter or Revoltress, p. 133.*

7. *See the poem headed Love of Comrades, p. 308.*

PREFACE TO
LEAVES OF GRASS.

America does not repel the past, or what it has produced under its forms, or amid other politics, or the idea of castes, or the old religions; accepts the lesson with calmness; is not so impatient as has been supposed that the slough still sticks to opinions and manners and literature while the life which served its requirements has passed into the new life of the new forms; perceives that the corpse is slowly borne from the eating and sleeping rooms of the house; perceives that it waits a little while in the door, that it was fittest for its days, that its action has descended to the stalwart and well-shaped heir who approaches, and that he shall be fittest for his days.

The Americans, of all nations at any time upon the earth, have probably the fullest poetical Nature. The United States themselves are essentially the greatest poem. In the history of the earth hitherto the largest and most stirring appear tame and orderly to their ampler largeness and stir. Here at last is something in the doings of man that corresponds with the broadcast doings of the day and night. Here is not merely a nation, but a teeming nation of nations. Here is action untied from strings, necessarily blind to particulars and details, magnificently moving in vast masses.

Here is the hospitality which for ever indicates heroes. Here are the roughs and beards and space and ruggedness and nonchalance that the soul loves. Here the performance, disdaining the trivial, unapproached in the tremendous audacity of its crowds and groupings and the push of its perspective, spreads with crampless and flowing breadth, and showers its prolific and splendid extravagance. One sees it must indeed own the riches of the summer and winter, and need never be bankrupt while corn grows from the ground, or the orchards drop apples, or the bays contain fish, or men beget children.

Other states indicate themselves in their deputies: but the genius of the United States is not best or most in its executives or legislatures, nor in its ambassadors or authors or colleges, or churches, or parlours, nor even in its newspapers or inventors, but always most in the common people. Their manners, speech, dress, friendships,—the freshness and candour of their physiognomy— the picturesque looseness of their carriage—their deathless attachment to freedom—their aversion to anything indecorous or soft or mean—the practical acknowledgment of the citizens of one state by the citizens of all other states—the fierceness of their roused resentment— their curiosity and welcome of novelty— their self-esteem and wonderful sympathy—their susceptibility to a slight—the air they have of persons who never knew how it felt to stand in the presence of superiors—the fluency of their speech—their delight in music, the sure symptom of manly tenderness and native elegance of soul—their good temper and open- handedness—the terrible significance of their elections, the President's taking off his hat to them, not they to him—these too are unrhymed poetry. It awaits the gigantic and generous treatment worthy of it.

The largeness of nature or the nation were monstrous without a corresponding largeness and generosity of the spirit of the citizen. Not nature, nor swarming states, nor streets and steamships, nor prosperous business, nor farms nor capital nor learning, may suffice for the ideal of man, nor suffice the poet. No reminiscences may suffice either. A live nation can always cut a deep mark, and can have the best authority the cheapest— namely, from its own soul. This is the sum of the profitable uses of individuals or states, and of present action and grandeur, and of the subjects of poets.—As if it were necessary to trot back generation after generation to the eastern records! As if the beauty and sacredness of the demonstrable must fall behind that of the mythical! As if men do not make their mark out of any times! As if the opening of the western continent by discovery, and what has transpired since in North and South America, were less than the small theatre of the antique, or the aimless sleep-walking of the Middle Ages! The pride of the United States leaves the wealth and finesse of the cities, and all returns of commerce and agriculture, and all the magnitude or geography or shows of exterior victory, to enjoy the breed of full-sized men, or one full-sized man unconquerable and simple.

The American poets are to enclose old and new; for America is the race of races. Of them a bard is to be commensurate with a people. To him the other continents arrive as contributions: he gives them reception for their sake and his own sake. His spirit responds to his country's spirit: he incarnates its geography and natural life and rivers and lakes. Mississippi with annual freshets and changing chutes, Missouri and Columbia and Ohio and Saint Lawrence with the Falls and beautiful masculine Hudson, do not embouchure where they spend themselves more than they embouchure into him. The blue breadth over the inland sea of Virginia and Maryland, and the sea off Massachusetts and Maine, and over Manhattan Bay, and over Champlain and Erie, and over Ontario and Huron and Michigan and Superior, and over the Texan and Mexican and Floridian and Cuban seas, and over the seas off California and Oregon, is not tallied by the blue breadth of the waters below more than the breadth of above and below is tallied by him. When the long Atlantic coast stretches longer, and the Pacific coast stretches longer, he easily stretches with them north or south. He spans between them also from east to west, and reflects what is between them. On him rise solid growths that offset the growths of pine and cedar and hemlock and live-oak and locust and chestnut and cypress and hickory and lime-tree and cottonwood and tulip-tree and cactus and wild-vine and tamarind and persimmon, and tangles as tangled as any cane-brake or swamp, and forests coated with transparent ice and icicles, hanging from the boughs and crackling in the wind, and sides and peaks of mountains, and pasturage sweet and free as savannah or upland or prairie,—with flights and songs and screams that answer those of the wild-pigeon and high-hold and orchard- oriole and coot and surf-duck and red-shouldered-bawk and fish-hawk and white-ibis and Indian-hen and cat-owl and water-pheasant and qua-bird and pied-sheldrake and blackbird and mocking-bird and buzzard and condor and night-heron and eagle. To him the hereditary countenance descends, both mother's and father's. To him enter the essences of the real things and past and present events— of the enormous diversity of temperature and agriculture and mines—the tribes of red aborigines—the weather-beaten vessels entering new ports, or making landings on rocky coasts—the first settlements north or south—the rapid stature and muscle— the haughty defiance of '76, and the war and peace and formation of the constitution— the union always surrounded by blatherers, and always calm and impregnable—the perpetual coming of immigrants—the wharf-hemmed cities and superior marine— the unsurveyed interior—the loghouses and clearings and wild animals and hunters and trappers—the free commerce—the fisheries and whaling and gold-digging—the endless gestations of new states—the convening of Congress every December, the members duly coming up from all climates and the uttermost parts—the noble character of the young mechanics and of all free American workmen and workwomen—the general ardour and friendliness and enterprise—the perfect equality of the female with the male—the large amativeness—the fluid movement of the population—the factories and mercantile life and labour-saving machinery— the Yankee swap—the New York firemen and the target excursion—the Southern plantation life—the character of the north-east and of the north- west and south-west-slavery, and the tremulous spreading of hands to protect it, and the stern opposition to it which shall never cease till it ceases, or the speaking of tongues and the moving of lips cease. For such the expression of the American poet is to be transcendent and new. It is to be indirect, and not direct or descriptive or epic. Its quality goes through these to much more. Let the age and wars of other nations be chanted, and their eras and characters be illustrated, and that finish the verse. Not so the great psalm of the republic. Here the theme is creative, and has vista. Here comes one among the well-beloved stone-cutters, and plans with decision and science, and sees the solid and beautiful forms of the future where there are now no solid forms.

Of all nations, the United States, with veins full of poetical stuff, most needs poets, and will doubtless have the greatest, and use them the greatest. Their Presidents shall not be their common referee so much as their poets shall. Of all mankind, the great poet is the equable man. Not in him, but off from him, things are grotesque or eccentric, or fail of their sanity. Nothing out of its place is good, and nothing in its place is bad. He bestows on every object or quality its fit proportions, neither more nor less. He is the arbiter of the diverse, and he is the key. He is the equaliser of his age and land: he supplies what wants supplying, and checks what wants checking. If peace is the routine, out of him speaks the spirit of peace, large, rich, thrifty, building vast and populous cities, encouraging agriculture and the arts and commerce—lighting the study of man, the soul, immortality—federal, state or municipal government, marriage, health, free-trade, intertravel by land and sea—nothing too close, nothing too far off,—the stars not too far off. In war, he is the most deadly force of the war. Who recruits him recruits horse and foot: he fetches parks of artillery, the best that engineer ever knew. If the time becomes slothful and heavy, he knows how to arouse it: he can make every word he speaks draw blood. Whatever stagnates in the flat of custom or obedience or legislation, he never stagnates. Obedience does not master him, he masters it. High up out of reach, he stands turning a concentrated light; he turns the pivot with his finger; he baffles the swiftest runners as he stands, and easily overtakes and envelops them. The time straying toward infidelity and confections and persiflage he withholds by his steady faith; he spreads out his dishes; he offers the sweet firm-fibred meat that grows men and women. His brain is the ultimate brain. He is no arguer, he is judgment. He judges not as the judge judges, but as the sun falling around a helpless thing. As he sees the farthest, he has the most faith. His thoughts are the hymns of the praise of things. In the talk on the soul and eternity and God, off of his equal plane, he is silent. He sees eternity less like a play with a prologue and denouement: he sees eternity in men and women,—he does not see men and women as dreams or dots. Faith is the antiseptic of the soul,—it pervades the common people and preserves them: they never give up believing and expecting and trusting. There is that indescribable freshness and unconsciousness about an illiterate person that humbles and mocks the power of the noblest expressive genius. The poet sees for a certainty how one not a great artist may be just as sacred and perfect as the greatest artist. The power to destroy or remould is freely used by him, but never the power of attack. What is past is past. If he does not expose superior models, and prove himself by every step he takes, he is not what is wanted. The presence of the greatest poet conquers; not parleying or struggling or any prepared attempts. Now he has passed that way, see after him! there is not left any vestige of despair or misanthropy or cunning or exclusiveness, or the ignominy of a nativity or colour, or delusion of hell or the necessity of hell; and no man thenceforward shall be degraded for ignorance or weakness or sin.

The greatest poet hardly knows pettiness or triviality. If he breathes into anything that was before thought small, it dilates with the grandeur and life of the universe. He is a seer—he is individual—he is complete in himself: the others are as good as he; only he sees it, and they do not. He is not one of the chorus—he does not stop for any regulation—he is the President of regulation. What the eyesight does to the rest he does to the rest. Who knows the curious mystery of the eyesight? The other senses corroborate themselves, but this is removed from any proof but its own, and foreruns the identities of the spiritual world. A single glance of it mocks all the investigations of man, and all the instruments and books of the earth, and all reasoning. What is marvellous? what is unlikely? what is impossible or baseless or vague? after you have once just opened the space of a peachpit, and given audience to far and near and to the sunset, and had all things enter with electric swiftness, softly and duly, without confusion or jostling or jam.

The land and sea, the animals, fishes, and birds, the sky of heaven and the orbs, the forests, mountains, and rivers, are not small themes: but folks expect of the poet to indicate more than the beauty and dignity which always attach to dumb real objects,—they expect him to indicate the path between reality and their souls. Men and women perceive the beauty well enough—probably as well as he. The passionate tenacity of hunters, woodmen, early risers, cultivators of gardens and orchards and fields, the love of healthy women for the manly form, seafaring persons, drivers of horses, the passion for light and the open air, all is an old varied sign of the unfailing perception of beauty, and of a residence of the poetic, in outdoor people. They can never be assisted by poets to perceive: some may, but they never can. The poetic quality is not marshalled in rhyme or uniformity, or abstract addresses to things, nor in melancholy complaints or good precepts, but is the life of these and much else, and is in the soul. The profit of rhyme is that it drops seeds of a sweeter and more luxuriant rhyme; and of uniformity, that it conveys itself into its own roots in the ground out of sight. The rhyme and uniformity of perfect poems show the free growth of metrical laws, and bud from them as unerringly and loosely as lilacs or roses on a bush, and take shapes as compact as the shapes of chestnuts and oranges and melons and pears, and shed the perfume impalpable to form. The fluency and ornaments of the finest poems or music or orations or recitations are not independent, but dependent. All beauty comes from beautiful blood and a beautiful brain. If the greatnesses are in conjunction in a man or woman, it is enough—the fact will prevail through the universe: but the gaggery and gilt of a million years will not prevail. Who troubles himself about his ornaments or fluency is lost. This is what you shall do: love the earth and sun and the animals, despise riches, give alms to every one that asks, stand up for the stupid and crazy, devote your income and labour to others, hate tyrants, argue not concerning God, have patience and indulgence towards the people, take off your hat to nothing known or unknown or to any man or number of men, go freely with powerful uneducated persons and with the young and with the mothers of families, read these leaves in the open air every season of every year of your life, re-examine all you have been told at school or church or in any book, dismiss whatever insults your own soul; and your very flesh shall be a great poem, and have the richest fluency, not only in its words, but in the silent lines of its lips and face, and between the lashes of your eyes, and in every motion and joint of your body. The poet shall not spend his time in unneeded work. He shall know that the ground is always ready ploughed and manured: others may not know it, but he shall. He shall go directly to the creation. His trust shall master the trust of everything he touches, and shall master all attachment.

The known universe has one complete lover, and that is the greatest poet. He consumes an eternal passion, and is indifferent which chance happens, and which possible contingency of fortune or misfortune, and persuades daily and hourly his delicious pay. What balks or breaks others is fuel for his burning progress to contact and amorous joy. Other proportions of the reception of pleasure dwindle to nothing to his proportions. All expected from heaven or from the highest he is rapport with in the sight of the daybreak, or a scene of the winter woods, or the presence of children playing, or with his arm round the neck of a man or woman. His love, above all love, has leisure and expanse—he leaves room ahead of himself. He is no irresolute or suspicious lover—he is sure—he scorns intervals. His experience and the showers and thrills are not for nothing. Nothing can jar him: suffering and darkness cannot—death and fear cannot. To him complaint and jealousy and envy are corpses buried and rotten in the earth—he saw them buried. The sea is not surer of the shore, or the shore of the sea, than he is of the fruition of his love, and of all perfection and beauty.

The fruition of beauty is no chance of hit or miss—it is inevitable as life—it is exact and plumb as gravitation. From the eyesight proceeds another eyesight, and from the hearing proceeds another hearing, and from the voice proceeds another voice, eternally curious of the harmony of things with man. To these respond perfections, not only in the committees that were supposed to stand for the rest, but in the rest themselves just the same. These understand the law of perfection in masses and floods—that its finish is to each for itself and onward from itself—that it is profuse and impartial—that there is not a minute of the light or dark, nor an acre of the earth or sea, without it—nor any direction of the sky, nor any trade or employment, nor any turn of events. This is the reason that about the proper expression of beauty there is precision and balance,—one part does not need to be thrust above another. The best singer is not the one who has the most lithe and powerful organ: the pleasure of poems is not in them that take the handsomest measure and similes and sound.

Without effort, and without exposing in the least how it is done, the greatest poet brings the spirit of any or all events and passions and scenes and persons, some more and some less, to bear on your individual character, as you hear or read. To do this well is to compete with the laws that pursue and follow time. What is the purpose must surely be there, and the clue of it must be there; and the faintest indication is the indication of the best, and then becomes the clearest indication. Past and present and future are not disjoined, but joined. The greatest poet forms the consistence of what is to be from what has been and is. He drags the dead out of their coffins, and stands them again on their feet: he says to the past, Rise and walk before me that I may realise you. He learns the lesson—he places himself where the future becomes present. The greatest poet does not only dazzle his rays over character and scenes and passions,—he finally ascends and finishes all: he exhibits the pinnacles that no man can tell what they are for or what is beyond—he glows a moment on the extremest verge. He is most wonderful in his last half-hidden smile or frown: by that flash of the moment of parting the one that sees it shall be encouraged or terrified afterward for many years. The greatest poet does not moralise or make applications of morals,—he knows the soul. The soul has that measureless pride which consists in never acknowledging any lessons but its own. But it has sympathy as measureless as its pride, and the one balances the other, and neither can stretch too far while it stretches in company with the other. The inmost secrets of art sleep with the twain. The greatest poet has lain close betwixt both, and they are vital in his style and thoughts.

The art of art, the glory of expression and the sunshine of the light of letters, is simplicity. Nothing is better than simplicity,—nothing can make up for excess or for the lack of definiteness. To carry on the heave of impulse, and pierce intellectual depths, and give all subjects their articulations, are powers neither common nor very uncommon. But to speak in literature with the perfect rectitude and insousiance of the movements of animals, and the unimpeachableness of the sentiment of trees in the woods and grass by the roadside, is the flawless triumph of art. If you, have looked on him who has achieved it, you have looked on one of the masters of the artists of all nations and times. You shall not contemplate the flight of the grey-gull over the bay, or the mettlesome action of the blood-horse, or the tall leaning of sunflowers on their stalk, or the appearance of the sun journeying through heaven, or the appearance of the moon afterward, with any more satisfaction than you shall contemplate him. The greatest poet has less a marked style, and is more the channel of thoughts and things without increase or diminution, and is the free channel of himself. He swears to his art,—I will not be meddlesome, I will not have in my writing any elegance or effect or originality to hang in the way between me and the rest like curtains. I will have nothing hang in the way, not the richest curtains. What I tell I tell for precisely what it is. Let who may exalt or startle or fascinate or soothe, I will have purposes as health or heat or snow has, and be as regardless of observation. What I experience or pourtray shall go from my composition without a shred of my composition. You shall stand by my side, and look in the mirror with me.

The old red blood and stainless gentility of great poets will be proved by their unconstraint. A heroic person walks at his ease through and out of that custom or precedent or authority that suits him not. Of the traits of the brotherhood of writers, savans, musicians, inventors, and artists, nothing is finer than silent defiance advancing from new free forms. In the need of poems, philosophy, politics, mechanism, science, behaviour, the craft of art, an appropriate native grand opera, shipcraft or any craft, he is greatest for ever and for ever who contributes the greatest original practical example. The cleanest expression is that which finds no sphere worthy of itself, and makes one.

The messages of great poets to each man and woman are,— Come to us on equal terms, only then can you understand us. We are no better than you; what we enclose you enclose, what we enjoy you may enjoy. Did you suppose there could be only one Supreme? We affirm there can be unnumbered Supremes, and that one does not countervail another any more than one eyesight countervails another—and that men can be good or grand only of the consciousness of their supremacy within them. What do you think is the grandeur of storms and dismemberments, and the deadliest battles and wrecks, and the wildest fury of the elements, and the power of the sea, and the motion of nature, and of the throes of human desires, and dignity and hate and love? It is that something in the soul which says,—Rage on, whirl on, I tread master here and everywhere; master of the spasms of the sky and of the shatter of the sea, master of nature and passion and death, and of all terror and all pain.

The American bards shall be marked for generosity and affection and for encouraging competitors: they shall be kosmos—without monopoly or secrecy—glad to pass anything to any one—hungry for equals night and day. They shall not be careful of riches and privilege,—they shall be riches and privilege: they shall perceive who the most affluent man is. The most affluent man is he that confronts all the shows he sees by equivalents out of the stronger wealth of himself. The American bard shall delineate no class of persons, nor one or two out of the strata of interests, nor love most nor truth most, nor the soul most nor the body most; and not be for the eastern states more than the western, or the northern states more than the southern.

Exact science and its practical movements are no checks on the greatest poet, but always his encouragement and support. The outset and remembrance are there—there the arms that lifted him first and brace him best—there he returns after all his goings and comings. The sailor and traveller, the anatomist, chemist, astronomer, geologist, phrenologist, spiritualist, mathematician, historian, and lexicographer, are not poets; but they are the lawgivers of poets, and their construction underlies the structure of every perfect poem. No matter what rises or is uttered, they send the seed of the conception of it: of them and by them stand the visible proofs of souls. If there shall be love and content between the father and the son, and if the greatness of the son is the exuding of the greatness of the father, there shall be love between the poet and the man of demonstrable science. In the beauty of poems are the tuft and final applause of science.

Great is the faith of the flush of knowledge, and of the investigation of the depths of qualities and things. Cleaving and circling here swells the soul of the poet: yet is president of itself always. The depths are fathomless, and therefore calm. The innocence and nakedness are resumed— they are neither modest nor immodest. The whole theory of the special and supernatural, and all that was twined with it or educed out of it, departs as a dream. What has ever happened, what happens, and whatever may or shall happen, the vital laws enclose all: they are sufficient for any case and for all cases—none to be hurried or retarded—any miracle of affairs or persons inadmissible in the vast clear scheme where every motion, and every spear of grass, and the frames and spirits of men and women, and all that concerns them, are unspeakably perfect miracles, all referring to all, and each distinct and in its place. It is also not consistent with the reality of the soul to admit that there is anything in the known universe more divine than men and women.

Men and women, and the earth and all upon it, are simply to be taken as they are, and the investigation of their past and present and future shall be unintermitted, and shall be done with perfect candour. Upon this basis philosophy speculates, ever looking toward the poet, ever regarding the eternal tendencies of all toward happiness, never inconsistent with what is clear to the senses and to the soul. For the eternal tendencies of all toward happiness make the only point of sane philosophy. Whatever comprehends less than that—whatever is less than the laws of light and of astronomical motion—or less than the laws that follow the thief, the liar, the glutton, and the drunkard, through this life, and doubtless afterward— or less than vast stretches of time, or the slow formation of density, or the patient upheaving of strata—is of no account. Whatever would put God in a poem or system of philosophy as contending against some being or influence is also of no account. Sanity and ensemble characterise the great master:—spoilt in one principle, all is spoilt. The great master has nothing to do with miracles. He sees health for himself in being one of the mass—he sees the hiatus in singular eminence. To the perfect shape comes common ground. To be under the general law is great, for that is to correspond with it. The master knows that he is unspeakably great, and that all are unspeakably great—that nothing, for instance, is greater than to conceive children, and bring them up well—that to be is just as great as to perceive or tell.

In the make of the great masters the idea of political liberty is indispensable. Liberty takes the adherence of heroes wherever men and women exist; but never takes any adherence or welcome from the rest more than from poets. They are the voice and exposition of liberty. They out of ages are worthy the grand idea,—to them it is confided, and they must sustain it. Nothing has precedence of it, and nothing can warp or degrade it. The attitude of great poets is to cheer up slaves and horrify despots. The turn of their necks, the sound of their feet, the motions of their wrists, are full of hazard to the one and hope to the other. Come nigh them a while, and, though they neither speak nor advise, you shall learn the faithful American lesson. Liberty is poorly served by men whose good intent is quelled from one failure or two failures or any number of failures, or from the casual indifference or ingratitude of the people, or from the sharp show of the tushes of power, or the bringing to bear soldiers and cannon or any penal statutes. Liberty relies upon itself, invites no one, promises nothing, sits in calmness and light, is positive and composed, and knows no discouragement. The battle rages with many a loud alarm and frequent advance and retreat—the enemy triumphs—the prison, the handcuffs, the iron necklace and anklet, the scaffold, garrote, and lead-balls, do their work— the cause is asleep—the strong throats are choked with their own blood—the young men drop their eyelashes toward the ground when they pass each other … and is liberty gone out of that place? No, never. When liberty goes, it is not the first to go, nor the second or third to go: it waits for all the rest to go— it is the last. When the memories of the old martyrs are faded utterly away—when the large names of patriots are laughed at in the public halls from the lips of the orators—when the boys are no more christened after the same, but christened after tyrants and traitors instead—when the laws of the free are grudgingly permitted, and laws for informers and blood-money are sweet to the taste of the people— when I and you walk abroad upon the earth, stung with compassion at the sight of numberless brothers answering our equal friendship, and calling no man master—and when we are elated with noble joy at the sight of slaves— when the soul retires in the cool communion of the night, and surveys its experience, and has much ecstasy over the word and deed that put back a helpless innocent person into the gripe of the gripers or into any cruel inferiority—when those in all parts of these states who could easier realise the true American character, but do not yet[1]—when the swarms of cringers, suckers, doughfaces, lice of politics, planners of sly involutions for their own preferment to city offices or state legislatures or the judiciary or Congress or the Presidency, obtain a response of love and natural deference from the people, whether they get the offices or no— when it is better to be a bound booby and rogue in office at a high salary than the poorest free mechanic or farmer, with his hat unmoved from his head, and firm eyes, and a candid and generous heart— and when servility by town or state or the federal government, or any oppression on a large scale or small scale, can be tried on without its own punishment following duly after in exact proportion, against the smallest chance of escape—or rather when all life and all the souls of men and women are discharged from any part of the earth—then only shall the instinct of liberty be discharged from that part of the earth.

[Footnote 1: This clause is obviously imperfect in some respect: it is here reproduced *verbatim* from the American edition.]

As the attributes of the poets of the kosmos concentre in the real body and soul and in the pleasure of things, they possess the superiority of genuineness over all fiction and romance. As they emit themselves, facts are showered over with light—the daylight is lit with more volatile light—also the deep between the setting and rising sun goes deeper many- fold. Each precise object or condition or combination or process exhibits a beauty: the multiplication-table its—old age its—the carpenter's trade its—the grand opera its: the huge-hulled clean-shaped New York clipper at sea under steam or full sail gleams with unmatched beauty—the American circles and large harmonies of government gleam with theirs, and the commonest definite intentions and actions with theirs. The poets of the kosmos advance through all interpositions and coverings and turmoils and stratagems to first principles. They are of use—they dissolve poverty from its need, and riches from its conceit. You large proprietor, they say, shall not realise or perceive more than any one else. The owner of the library is not he who holds a legal title to it, having bought and paid for it. Any one and every one is owner of the library who can read the same through all the varieties of tongues and subjects and styles, and in whom they enter with ease, and take residence and force toward paternity and maternity, and make supple and powerful and rich and large. These American states, strong and healthy and accomplished, shall receive no pleasure from violations of natural models, and must not permit them. In paintings or mouldings or carvings in mineral or wood, or in the illustrations of books or newspapers, or in any comic or tragic prints, or in the patterns of woven stuffs, or anything to beautify rooms or furniture or costumes, or to put upon cornices or monuments or on the prows or sterns of ships, or to put anywhere before the human eye indoors or out, that which distorts honest shapes, or which creates unearthly beings or places or contingencies, is a nuisance and revolt. Of the human form especially, it is so great it must never be made ridiculous. Of ornaments to a work, nothing *outré* can be allowed; but those ornaments can be allowed that conform to the perfect facts of the open air, and that flow out of the nature of the work, and come irrepressibly from it, and are necessary to the completion of the work. Most works are most beautiful without ornament. Exaggerations will be revenged in human physiology. Clean and vigorous children are conceived only in those communities where the models of natural forms are public every day. Great genius and the people of these states must never be demeaned to romances. As soon as histories are properly told, there is no more need of romances.

The great poets are also to be known by the absence in them of tricks, and by the justification of perfect personal candour. Then folks echo a new cheap joy and a divine voice leaping from their brains. How beautiful is candour! All faults may be forgiven of him who has perfect candour. Henceforth let no man of us lie, for we have seen that openness wins the inner and outer world, and that there is no single exception, and that never since our earth gathered itself in a mass has deceit or subterfuge or prevarication attracted its smallest particle or the faintest tinge of a shade—and that through the enveloping wealth and rank of a state or the whole republic of states a sneak or sly person shall be discovered and despised—and that the soul has never been once fooled and never can be fooled—and thrift without the loving nod of the soul is only a foetid puff—and there never grew up in any of the continents of the globe, nor upon any planet or satellite or star, nor upon the asteroids, nor in any part of ethereal space, nor in the midst of density, nor under the fluid wet of the sea, nor in that condition which precedes the birth of babes, nor at any time during the changes of life, nor in that condition that follows what we term death, nor in any stretch of abeyance or action afterward of vitality, nor in any process of formation or reformation anywhere, a being whose instinct hated the truth.

Extreme caution or prudence, the soundest organic health, large hope and comparison and fondness for women and children, large alimentiveness and destructiveness and causality, with a perfect sense of the oneness of nature, and the propriety of the same spirit applied to human affairs— these are called up of the float of the brain of the world to be parts of the greatest poet from his birth. Caution seldom goes far enough. It has been thought that the prudent citizen was the citizen who applied himself to solid gains, and did well for himself and his family, and completed a lawful life without debt or crime. The greatest poet sees and admits these economies as he sees the economies of food and sleep, but has higher notions of prudence than to think he gives much when he gives a few slight attentions at the latch of the gate. The premises of the prudence of life are not the hospitality of it, or the ripeness and harvest of it. Beyond the independence of a little sum laid aside for burial-money, and of a few clapboards around and shingles overhead on a lot of American soil owned, and the easy dollars that supply the year's plain clothing and meals, the melancholy prudence of the abandonment of such a great being as a man is to the toss and pallor of years of money-making, with all their scorching days and icy nights, and all their stifling deceits and underhanded dodgings, or infinitesimals of parlours, or shameless stuffing while others starve,—and all the loss of the bloom and odour of the earth, and of the flowers and atmosphere, and of the sea, and of the true taste of the women and men you pass or have to do with in youth or middle age, and the issuing sickness and desperate revolt at the close of a life without elevation or naïveté, and the ghastly chatter of a death without serenity or majesty,—is the great fraud upon modern civilisation and forethought; blotching the surface and system which civilisation undeniably drafts, and moistening with tears the immense features it spreads and spreads with such velocity before the reached kisses of the soul. Still the right explanation remains to be made about prudence. The prudence of the mere wealth and respectability of the most esteemed life appears too faint for the eye to observe at all when little and large alike drop quietly aside at the thought of the prudence suitable for immortality. What is wisdom that fills the thinness of a year or seventy or eighty years, to wisdom spaced out by ages, and coming back at a certain time with strong reinforcements and rich presents and the clear faces of wedding-guests as far as you can look in every direction running gaily toward you? Only the soul is of itself—all else has reference to what ensues. All that a person does or thinks is of consequence. Not a move can a man or woman make that affects him or her in a day or a month, or any part of the direct lifetime or the hour of death, but the same affects him or her onward afterward through the indirect lifetime. The indirect is always as great and real as the direct. The spirit receives from the body just as much as it gives to the body. Not one name of word or deed—not of the putrid veins of gluttons or rum-drinkers— not peculation or cunning or betrayal or murder—no serpentine poison of those that seduce women—not the foolish yielding of women—not of the attainment of gain by discreditable means— not any nastiness of appetite— not any harshness of officers to men, or judges to prisoners, or fathers to sons, or sons to fathers, or of husbands to wives, or bosses to their boys—not of greedy looks or malignant wishes—nor any of the wiles practised by people upon themselves—ever is or ever can be stamped on the programme, but it is duly realised and returned, and that returned in further performances, and they returned again. Nor can the push of charity or personal force ever be anything else than the profoundest reason, whether it bring arguments to hand or no. No specification is necessary—to add or subtract or divide is in vain. Little or big, learned or unlearned, white or black, legal or illegal, sick or well, from the first inspiration down the windpipe to the last expiration out of it, all that a male or female does that is vigorous and benevolent and clean is so much sure profit to him or her in the unshakable order of the universe and through the whole scope of it for ever. If the savage or felon is wise, it is well—if the greatest poet or savant is wise, it is simply the same—if the President or chief justice is wise, it is the same—if the young mechanic or farmer is wise, it is no more or less. The interest will come round—all will come round. All the best actions of war and peace—all help given to relatives and strangers, and the poor and old and sorrowful, and young children and widows and the sick, and to all shunned persons— all furtherance of fugitives and of the escape of slaves—all the self-denial that stood steady and aloof on wrecks, and saw others take the seats of the boats—all offering of substance or life for the good old cause, or for a friend's sake or opinion's sake—all pains of enthusiasts scoffed at by their neighbours—all the vast sweet love and precious suffering of mothers—all honest men baffled in strifes recorded or unrecorded—all the grandeur and good of the few ancient nations whose fragments of annals we inherit—and all the good of the hundreds of far mightier and more ancient nations unknown to us by name or date or location—all that was ever manfully begun, whether it succeeded or no—all that has at any time been well suggested out of the divine heart of man, or by the divinity of his mouth, or by the shaping of his great hands—and all that is well thought or done this day on any part of the surface of the globe, or on any of the wandering stars or fixed stars by those there as we are here—or that is henceforth to be well thought or done by you, whoever you are, or by any one—these singly and wholly inured at their time, and inured now, and will inure always, to the identities from which they sprung or shall spring. Did you guess any of them lived only its moment? The world does not so exist— no parts, palpable or impalpable, so exist—no result exists now without being from its long antecedent result, and that from its antecedent, and so backward without the farthest mentionable spot coining a bit nearer the beginning than any other spot…. Whatever satisfies the soul is truth. The prudence of the greatest poet answers at last the craving and glut of the soul, is not contemptuous of less ways of prudence if they conform to its ways, puts off nothing, permits no let-up for its own case or any case, has no particular Sabbath or judgment-day, divides not the living from the dead or the righteous from the unrighteous, is satisfied with the present, matches every thought or act by its correlative, knows no possible forgiveness or deputed atonement—knows that the young man who composedly perilled his life and lost it has done exceeding well for himself, while the man who has not perilled his life, and retains it to old age in riches and ease, has perhaps achieved nothing for himself worth mentioning—and that only that person has no great prudence to learn who has learnt to prefer long-lived things, and favours body and soul the same, and perceives the indirect assuredly following the direct, and what evil or good he does leaping onward and waiting to meet him again—and who in his spirit in any emergency whatever neither hurries nor avoids death.

The direct trial of him who would be the greatest poet is to-day. If he does not flood himself with the immediate age as with vast oceanic tides— and if he does not attract his own land body and soul to himself, and hang on its neck with incomparable love— and if he be not himself the age transfigured—and if to him is not opened the eternity which gives similitude to all periods and locations and processes and animate and inanimate forms, and which is the bond of time, and rises up from its inconceivable vagueness and infiniteness in the swimming shape of to-day, and is held by the ductile anchors of life, and makes the present spot the passage from what was to what shall be, and commits itself to the representation of this wave of an hour, and this one of the sixty beautiful children of the wave—let him merge in the general run and wait his development.... Still, the final test of poems or any character or work remains. The prescient poet projects himself centuries ahead, and judges performer or performance after the changes of time. Does it live through them? Does it still hold on untired? Will the same style, and the direction of genius to similar points, be satisfactory now? Has no new discovery in science, or arrival at superior planes of thought and judgment and behaviour, fixed him or his so that either can be looked down upon? Have the marches of tens and hundreds and thousands of years made willing detours to the right hand and the left hand for his sake? Is he beloved long and long after he is buried? Does the young man think often of him? and the young woman think often of him? and do the middle-aged and the old think of him?

A great poem is for ages and ages, in common, and for all degrees and complexions, and all departments and sects, and for a woman as much as a man, and a man as much as a woman. A great poem is no finish to a man or woman, but rather a beginning. Has any one fancied he could sit at last under some due authority, and rest satisfied with explanations, and realise and be content and full? To no such terminus does the greatest poet bring— he brings neither cessation nor sheltered fatness and ease. The touch of him tells in action. Whom he takes he takes with firm sure grasp into live regions previously unattained. Thenceforward is no rest: they see the space and ineffable sheen that turn the old spots and lights into dead vacuums. The companion of him beholds the birth and progress of stars, and learns one of the meanings. Now there shall be a man cohered out of tumult and chaos. The elder encourages the younger, and shows him how: they two shall launch off fearlessly together till the new world fits an orbit for itself, and looks unabashed on the lesser orbits of the stars, and sweeps through the ceaseless rings, and shall never be quiet again.

There will soon be no more priests. Their work is done. They may wait a while—perhaps a generation or two,—dropping off by degrees. A superior breed shall take their place—the gangs of kosmos and prophets *en masse* shall take their place. A new order shall arise; and they shall be the priests of man, and every man shall be his own priest. The churches built under their umbrage shall be the churches of men and women. Through the divinity of themselves shall the kosmos and the new breed of poets be interpreters of men and women and of all events and things. They shall find their inspiration in real objects to-day, symptoms of the past and future. They shall not deign to defend immortality, or God, or the perfection of things, or liberty, or the exquisite beauty and reality of the soul. They shall arise in America, and be responded to from the remainder of the earth.

The English language befriends the grand American expression—it is brawny enough, and limber and full enough. On the tough stock of a race who, through all change of circumstance, was never without the idea of political liberty, which is the animus of all liberty, it has attracted the terms of daintier and gayer and subtler and more elegant tongues. It is the powerful language of resistance—it is the dialect of common sense. It is the speech of the proud and melancholy races, and of all who aspire. It is the chosen tongue to express growth, faith, self-esteem, freedom, justice, equality, friendliness, amplitude, prudence, decision, and courage. It is the medium that shall well nigh express the inexpressible.

No great literature, nor any like style of behaviour or oratory or social intercourse or household arrangements or public institutions, or the treatment by bosses of employed people, nor executive detail, or detail of the army or navy, nor spirit of legislation, or courts or police, or tuition or architecture, or songs or amusements, or the costumes of young men, can long elude the jealous and passionate instinct of American standards. Whether or no the sign appears from the mouths of the people, it throbs a live interrogation in every freeman's and freewoman's heart after that which passes by, or this built to remain. Is it uniform with my country? Are its disposals without ignominious distinctions? Is it for the ever-growing communes of brothers and lovers, large, well united, proud beyond the old models, generous beyond all models? Is it something grown fresh out of the fields, or drawn from the sea, for use to me, to-day, here? I know that what answers for me, an American, must answer for any individual or nation that serves for a part of my materials. Does this answer? or is it without reference to universal needs? or sprung of the needs of the less developed society of special ranks? or old needs of pleasure overlaid by modern science and forms? Does this acknowledge liberty with audible and absolute acknowledgment, and set slavery at nought, for life and death? Will it help breed one good-shaped man, and a woman to be his perfect and independent mate? Does it improve manners? Is it for the nursing of the young of the republic? Does it solve readily with the sweet milk of the breasts of the mother of many children? Has it too the old, ever-fresh forbearance and impartiality? Does it look with the same love on the last-born and on those hardening toward stature, and on the errant, and on those who disdain all strength of assault outside of their own?

The poems distilled from other poems will probably pass away. The coward will surely pass away. The expectation of the vital and great can only be satisfied by the demeanour of the vital and great. The swarms of the polished, deprecating, and reflectors, and the polite, float off and leave no remembrance. America prepares with composure and goodwill for the visitors that have sent word. It is not intellect that is to be their warrant and welcome. The talented, the artist, the ingenious, the editor, the statesman, the erudite—they are not unappreciated—they fall in their place and do their work. The soul of the nation also does its work. No disguise can pass on it—no disguise can conceal from it. It rejects none, it permits all. Only toward as good as itself and toward the like of itself will it advance half-way. An individual is as superb as a nation when he has the qualities which make a superb nation. The soul of the largest and wealthiest and proudest nation may well go half-way to meet that of its poets. The signs are effectual. There is no fear of mistake. If the one is true, the other is true. The proof of a poet is that his country absorbs him as affectionately as he has absorbed it.

"Meantime, dear friend, Farewell, Walt Whitman."

CHANTS DEMOCRATIC.

STARTING FROM PAUMANOK.

1.

Starting from fish-shape Paumanok,[1] where I was born,
Well-begotten, and raised by a perfect mother;
After roaming many lands—lover of populous pavements;
Dweller in Mannahatta,[2] city of ships, my city,—or on
    southern savannas;
Or a soldier camped, or carrying my knapsack and gun—
    or a miner inCalifornia;
Or rude in my home in Dakotah's woods, my diet meat,
    my drink from the spring;
Or withdrawn to muse and meditate in some deep recess,
Far from the clank of crowds, intervals passing, rapt and
    happy;
Aware of the fresh free giver, the flowing Missouri—aware
    of mighty Niagara
Aware of the buffalo herds, grazing the plains—the
    hirsute and strong-breasted bull;
Of earths, rocks, fifth-month flowers, experienced—stars,
    rain, snow, my amaze;
Having studied the mocking-bird's tones, and the
    mountain hawk's,
And heard at dusk the unrivalled one, the hermit thrush,
    from the swamp-cedars,
Solitary, singing in the West, I strike up for a New World.

2.

Victory, union, faith, identity, time,

Yourself, the present and future lands, the indissoluble
    compacts, riches, mystery,
Eternal progress, the kosmos, and the modern reports.

This, then, is life;
Here is what has come to the surface after so many throes
    and convulsions.

How curious! how real!
Under foot the divine soil—over head the sun.

See, revolving, the globe;
The ancestor-continents, away, grouped together;
The present and future continents, north and south, with
    the isthmus between.

See, vast trackless spaces;
As in a dream, they change, they swiftly fill;
Countless masses debouch upon them;
They are now covered with the foremost people, arts,
    institutions, known.

See, projected through time,
For me an audience interminable.

With firm and regular step they wend—they never stop,
Successions of men, Americanos, a hundred millions;
One generation playing its part, and passing on,
Another generation playing its part, and passing on in its
    turn,
With faces turned sideways or backward towards me, to
    listen,
With eyes retrospective towards me.

3.

Americanos! conquerors! marches humanitarian;
Foremost! century marches! Libertad! masses!
For you a programme of chants.

Chants of the prairies;
Chants of the long-running Mississippi, and down to the
        Mexican Sea;
Chants of Ohio, Indiana, Illinois, Iowa, Wisconsin, and
        Minnesota;
Chants going forth from the centre, from Kansas, and
        thence, equidistant,
Shooting in pulses of fire, ceaseless, to vivify all.

4.

In the Year 80 of the States,[3]
My tongue, every atom of my blood, formed from this
        soil, this air,
Born here of parents born here, from parents the same,
        and their parents the same,
I, now thirty-six years old, in perfect health begin,
Hoping to cease not till death.

Creeds and schools in abeyance,
(Retiring back a while, sufficed at what they are, but never
        forgotten.)
I harbour, for good or bad—I permit to speak, at every
        hazard—
Nature now without check, with original energy.

5.

Take my leaves, America! take them South, and take them
    North!
Make welcome for them everywhere, for they are your
    own offspring;
Surround them, East and West! for they would surround
    you;
And you precedents! connect lovingly with them, for they
    connect lovingly with you.

I conned old times;
I sat studying at the feet of the great masters:
Now, if eligible, O that the great masters might return and
    study me!

In the name of these States, shall I scorn the antique?
Why, these are the children of the antique, to justify it.

6.

Dead poets, philosophs, priests,
Martyrs, artists, inventors, governments long since,
Language-shapers on other shores,
Nations once powerful, now reduced, withdrawn, or
    desolate,
I dare not proceed till I respectfully credit what you have
    left, wafted hither:
I have perused it—own it is admirable, (moving awhile
    among it;)
Think nothing can ever be greater—nothing can ever
    deserve more than it deserves;
Regarding it all intently a long while, then dismissing it,
I stand in my place, with my own day, here.

Here lands female and male;
Here the heirship and heiress-ship of the world—here the
    flame of materials;
Here spirituality, the translatress, the openly-avowed,
The ever-tending, the finale of visible forms;
The satisfier, after due long-waiting, now advancing,
Yes, here comes my mistress, the Soul.

7.

The SOUL! For ever and for ever—longer than soil is
    brown and solid—longer than water ebbs and flows.

I will make the poems of materials, for I think they are to
    be the most spiritual poems;
And I will make the poems of my body and of mortality,
For I think I shall then supply myself with the poems of
    my soul, and of immortality.

I will make a song for these States, that no one State may
    under any circumstances be subjected to another
    State;
And I will make a song that there shall be comity by day
    and by night between all the States, and between any
    two of them;

And I will make a song for the ears of the President, full
    of weapons with menacing points,
And behind the weapons countless dissatisfied faces:
And a song make I, of the One formed out of all;
The fanged and glittering one whose head is over all;
Resolute, warlike one, including and over all;
However high the head of any else, that head is over all.

I will acknowledge contemporary lands;

I will trail the whole geography of the globe, and salute
    courteously every city large and small;
And employments! I will put in my poems, that with you
    is heroism, upon land and sea—And I will report all
    heroism from an American point of view;
And sexual organs and acts! do you concentrate in me—
    for I am determined to tell you with courageous clear
    voice, to prove you illustrious.

I will sing the song of companionship;
I will show what alone must finally compact these;
I believe These are to found their own ideal of manly love,
    indicating it in me;
I will therefore let flame from me the burning fires that
    were threatening to consume me;

I will lift what has too long kept down those smouldering
    fires;
I will give them complete abandonment;
I will write the evangel-poem of comrades and of love;
For who but I should understand love, with all its sorrow
    and joy?
And who but I should be the poet of comrades?

8.

I am the credulous man of qualities, ages, races;
I advance from the people *en masse* in their own spirit;
Here is what sings unrestricted faith.

Omnes! Omnes! let others ignore what they may;
I make the poem of evil also—I commemorate that part
    also;
I am myself just as much evil as good, and my nation is—
    And I say there is in fact no evil,

Or if there is, I say it is just as important to you, to the
    land, or to me, as anything else.

I too, following many, and followed by many, inaugurate a
    Religion—I too go to the wars;
It may be I am destined to utter the loudest cries thereof,
    the winner's pealing shouts;
Who knows? they may rise from me yet, and soar above
    everything.

Each is not for its own sake; I say the whole earth, and all
    the stars in the sky, are for religion's sake.

I say no man has ever yet been half devout enough;
None has ever yet adored or worshipped half enough;
None has begun to think how divine he himself is, and
    how certain the future is.

I say that the real and permanent grandeur of these States
    must be their religion;
Otherwise there is no real and permanent grandeur;
Nor character, nor life worthy the name, without religion;
Nor land, nor man or woman, without religion.

9.

What are you doing, young man?
Are you so earnest—so given up to literature, science, art,
    amours?
These ostensible realities, politics, points?
Your ambition or business, whatever it may be?

It is well—Against such I say not a word—I am their poet
    also;

But behold! such swiftly subside—burnt up for religion's
    sake;
For not all matter is fuel to heat, impalpable flame, the
    essential life of the earth,
Any more than such are to religion.

10.

What do you seek, so pensive and silent?
What do you need, Camerado?

Dear son! do you think it is love?
Listen, dear son—listen, America, daughter or son! It is a
    painful thing to love a man or woman to excess—and
    yet it satisfies—it is great;
But there is something else very great—it makes the whole
    coincide;
It, magnificent, beyond materials, with continuous hands,
    sweeps and provides for all.

11.

Know you: to drop in the earth the germs of a greater
    religion,
The following chants, each for its kind, I sing.

My comrade!
For you, to share with me, two greatnesses—and a third
    one, rising inclusive and more resplendent,
The greatness of Love and Democracy—and the greatness
    of Religion.

Mélange mine own! the unseen and the seen;
Mysterious ocean where the streams empty;

Prophetic spirit of materials shifting and flickering
    around me;
Living beings, identities, now doubtless near us in the air,
    that we know not of;
Contact daily and hourly that will not release me;
These selecting—these, in hints, demanded of me.

Not he with a daily kiss onward from childhood kissing
    me
Has winded and twisted around me that which holds me
    to him,
Any more than I am held to the heavens, to the spiritual
    world,
And to the identities of the Gods, my lovers, faithful and
    true,
After what they have done to me, suggesting themes.

O such themes! Equalities!
O amazement of things! O divine average!
O warblings under the sun—ushered, as now, or at noon,
    or setting!
O strain, musical, flowing through ages—now reaching
    hither,
I take to your reckless and composite chords—I add to
    them, and cheerfully pass them forward.

12.

As I have walked in Alabama my morning walk,
I have seen where the she-bird, the mocking-bird, sat on
    her nest in the briars, hatching her brood.

I have seen the he-bird also;
I have paused to hear him, near at hand, inflating his
    throat, and joyfully singing.

And while I paused, it came to me that what he really
    sang for was not there only,
Nor for his mate nor himself only, nor all sent back by the
    echoes;
But subtle, clandestine, away beyond,
A charge transmitted, and gift occult, for those being
    born.

13.

Democracy!
Near at hand to you a throat is now inflating itself and
    joyfully singing.

Ma femme!
For the brood beyond us and of us,
For those who belong here, and those to come,
I, exultant, to be ready for them, will now shake out carols
    stronger and haughtier than have ever yet been heard
    upon earth.

I will make the songs of passion, to give them their way,
    And your songs, outlawed offenders—for I scan you
    with kindred eyes, and carry you with me the same as
    any.

I will make the true poem of riches,— To earn for the
    body and the mind whatever adheres, and goes
    forward, and is not dropped by death.

I will effuse egotism, and show it underlying all—and I
    will be the bard of personality;
And I will show of male and female that either is but the
    equal of the other;

And I will show that there is no imperfection in the
      present—and can be none in the future;
And I will show that, whatever happens to anybody, it
      may be turned to beautiful results—and I will show
      that nothing can happen more beautiful than death;
And I will thread a thread through my poems that time
      and events are compact,
And that all the things of the universe are perfect
      miracles, each as profound as any.

I will not make poems with reference to parts;
But I will make leaves, poems, poemets, songs, says,
      thoughts, with reference to ensemble:
And I will not sing with reference to a day, but with
      reference to all days;
And I will not make a poem, nor the least part of a poem,
      but has reference to the soul;
Because, having looked at the objects of the universe, I
      find there is no one, nor any particle of one, but has
      reference to the soul.

14.

Was somebody asking to see the Soul?
See! your own shape and countenance—persons,
      substances, beasts, the trees, the running rivers, the
      rocks and sands.

All hold spiritual joys, and afterwards loosen them:
How can the real body ever die, and be buried?

Of your real body, and any man's or woman's real body,
Item for item, it will elude the hands of the corpse-
      cleaners, and pass to fitting spheres,

Carrying what has accrued to it from the moment of birth
    to the moment of death.

Not the types set up by the printer return their
    impression, the meaning, the main concern,
Any more than a man's substance and life, or a woman's
    substance and life, return in the body and the soul,
Indifferently before death and after death.

Behold! the body includes and is the meaning, the main
    concern—and includes and is the soul; Whoever you
    are! how superb and how divine is your body, or any
    part of it.

15.

Whoever you are! to you endless announcements.

Daughter of the lands, did you wait for your poet?
Did you wait for one with a flowing mouth and indicative
    hand?

Toward the male of the States, and toward the female of
    the States,
Live words—words to the lands.
O the lands! interlinked, food-yielding lands!
Land of coal and iron! Land of gold! Lands of cotton,
    sugar, rice!
Land of wheat, beef, pork! Land of wool and hemp! Land
    of the apple and grape!
Land of the pastoral plains, the grass-fields of the world!
    Land of those sweet-aired interminable plateaus!
Land of the herd, the garden, the healthy house of adobie!
Lands where the north-west Columbia winds, and where
    the south-west Colorado winds!

Land of the eastern Chesapeake! Land of the Delaware!
Land of Ontario, Erie, Huron, Michigan!
Land of the Old Thirteen! Massachusetts land! Land of
    Vermont and Connecticut!
Land of the ocean shores! Land of sierras and peaks!
Land of boatmen and sailors! Fishermen's land!
Inextricable lands! the clutched together! the passionate
    ones!
The side by side! the elder and younger brothers! the
    bony-limbed!
The great women's land! the feminine! the experienced
    sisters and the inexperienced sisters!
Far-breathed land! Arctic-braced! Mexican-breezed! the
    diverse! the compact!
The Pennsylvanian! the Virginian! the double Carolinian!
O all and each well-loved by me! my intrepid nations! O I
    at any rate
include you all with perfect love!
I cannot be discharged from you—not from one, any
    sooner than another!

O Death! O!—for all that, I am yet of you unseen, this
    hour, with irrepressible love,
Walking New England, a friend, a traveller,
Splashing my bare feet in the edge of the summer ripples,
    on Paumanok's sands,
Crossing the prairies—dwelling again in Chicago—
    dwelling in every town,
Observing shows, births, improvements, structures, arts,
Listening to the orators and the oratresses in public halls,
Of and through the States, as during life[4]—each man and
    woman my neighbour,
The Louisianian, the Georgian, as near to me, and I as
    near to him and her,

The Mississippian and Arkansian yet with me—and I yet
    with any of them;
Yet upon the plains west of the spinal river—yet in my
    house of adobie,
Yet returning eastward—yet in the Sea-Side State, or in
    Maryland,
Yet Canadian cheerily braving the winter—the snow and
    ice welcome to me, or mounting the Northern Pacific,
    to Sitka, to Aliaska;
Yet a true son either of Maine, or of the Granite State,[5] or
    of the Narragansett Bay State, or of the Empire State;[6]
Yet sailing to other shores to annex the same—yet
    welcoming every new brother;
Hereby applying these leaves to the new ones, from the
    hour they unite with the old ones;
Coming among the new ones myself, to be their
    companion and equal—coming personally to you
    now;
Enjoining you to acts, characters, spectacles, with me.

16.

With me, with firm holding—yet haste, haste on.

For your life, adhere to me;
Of all the men of the earth, I only can unloose you and
    toughen you;
I may have to be persuaded many times before I consent
    to give myself to you—but what of that?
Must not Nature be persuaded many times?
No dainty *dolce affettuoso* I;
Bearded, sunburnt, gray-necked, forbidding, I have
    arrived,
To be wrestled with as I pass, for the solid prizes of the
    universe;

For such I afford whoever can persevere to win them.

17.

On my way a moment I pause;
Here for you! and here for America!
Still the Present I raise aloft—still the Future of the States
    I harbinge, glad and sublime;
And for the Past, I pronounce what the air holds of the
    red aborigines.

The red aborigines!
Leaving natural breaths, sounds of rain and winds, calls
    as of birds and animals in the woods, syllabled to us
    for names; Okonee, Koosa, Ottawa, Monongahela,
    Sauk, Natchez, Chattahoochee, Kaqueta, Oronoco,
Wabash, Miami, Saginaw, Chippewa, Oshkosh, Walla-
    Walla;
Leaving such to the States, they melt, they depart,
    charging the water and the land with names.

18.

O expanding and swift! O henceforth,
Elements, breeds, adjustments, turbulent, quick, and
    audacious;
A world primal again—vistas of glory, incessant and
    branching;
A new race, dominating previous ones, and grander far,
    with new contests,
New politics, new literatures and religions, new
    inventions and arts.

These my voice announcing—I will sleep no more, but
    arise;

You oceans that have been calm within me! how I feel
    you, fathomless, stirring, preparing unprecedented
    waves and storms.

19.

See! steamers steaming through my poems!
See in my poems immigrants continually coming and
    landing;
See in arriere, the wigwam, the trail, the hunter's hut, the
    flat-boat, the maize-leaf, the claim, the rude fence,
    and the backwoods village;
See, on the one side the Western Sea, and on the other the
    Eastern Sea, how they advance and retreat upon my
    poems, as upon their own shores;
See pastures and forests in my poems—See animals, wild
    and tame—See, beyond the Kanzas, countless herds of
    buffalo, feeding on short curly grass;
See, in my poems, cities, solid, vast, inland, with paved
    streets, with iron and stone edifices, ceaseless vehicles,
    and commerce;
See the many-cylindered steam printing-press—See the
    electric telegraph, stretching across the Continent,
    from the Western Sea to Manhattan;
See, through Atlantica's depths, pulses American, Europe
    reaching—pulses of Europe, duly returned;
See the strong and quick locomotive, as it departs,
    panting, blowing the steam-whistle;
See ploughmen, ploughing farms—See miners, digging
    mines—See the numberless factories;
See mechanics, busy at their benches, with tools—See,
    from among them, superior judges, philosophs,
    Presidents, emerge, dressed in working dresses;
See, lounging through the shops and fields of the States,
    me, well-beloved, close-held by day and night;

Hear the loud echoes of my songs there! Read the hints
    come at last.

20.

O Camerado close!
O you and me at last—and us two only.
O a word to clear one's path ahead endlessly!
O something ecstatic and undemonstrable! O music wild!
O now I triumph—and you shall also;
O hand in hand—O wholesome pleasure—O one more
    desirer and lover!
O to haste, firm holding—to haste, haste on, with me.

FOOTNOTES :

1. *Paumanok is the native name of Long Island, State of New York.
   It presents a fish-like shape on the map.*
2. *Mannahatta, or Manhattan, is (as many readers will
   know) New York.*
3. *1856.*
4. *The poet here contemplates himself as yet living spiritually and in
   his poems after the death of the body, still a friend and brother to
   all present and future American lands and persons.*
5. *New Hampshire.*
6. *New York State.*

AMERICAN FEUILLAGE.

AMERICA always!
Always our own feuillage!
Always Florida's green peninsula! Always the priceless
  delta of Louisiana!
Always the cotton-fields of Alabama and Texas!
Always California's golden hills and hollows—and
    the silver mountains of New Mexico! Always soft-
    breathed Cuba!
Always the vast slope drained by the Southern Sea—
    inseparable with the slopes drained by the Eastern
    and Western Seas!
The area the eighty-third year of these States[1]—the three
    and a half millions of square miles;
The eighteen thousand miles of sea-coast and bay-coast
    on the main—the thirty thousand miles of river
    navigation,
The seven millions of distinct families, and the same
    number of dwellings—
Always these, and more, branching forth into numberless
    branches;
Always the free range and diversity! Always the continent
    of Democracy!
Always the prairies, pastures, forests, vast cities, travellers,
    Canada, the snows;
Always these compact lands—lands tied at the hips with
    the belt stringing the huge oval lakes;
Always the West, with strong native persons—the
    increasing density there— the habitans, friendly,
    threatening, ironical, scorning invaders;

All sights, South, North, East—all deeds, promiscuously
    done at all times,
All characters, movements, growths—a few noticed,
    myriads unnoticed.
Through Mannahatta's streets I walking, these things
    gathering.
On interior rivers, by night, in the glare of pine knots,
    steamboats wooding up:
Sunlight by day on the valley of the Susquehanna, and on
    the valleys of the
Potomac and Rappahannock, and the valleys of the
    Roanoke and Delaware;
In their northerly wilds beasts of prey haunting the
    Adirondacks the hills—or lapping the Saginaw waters
    to drink;
In a lonesome inlet, a sheldrake, lost from the flock,
    sitting on the water, rocking silently;
In farmers' barns, oxen in the stable, their harvest labour
    done—they rest standing—they are too tired;
Afar on arctic ice, the she-walrus lying drowsily, while her
    cubs play around;
The hawk sailing where men have not yet sailed—the
    farthest polar sea, ripply, crystalline, open, beyond the
    floes;
White drift spooning ahead, where the ship in the
    tempest dashes.
On solid land, what is done in cities, as the bells all strike
    midnight together;
In primitive woods, the sounds there also sounding—the
    howl of the wolf, the scream of the panther, and the
    hoarse bellow of the elk;
In winter beneath the hard blue ice of Moosehead Lake,
    in summer visible through the clear waters, the great
    trout swimming;

In lower latitudes, in warmer air, in the Carolinas, the
    large black buzzard floating slowly, high beyond the
    tree-tops,
Below, the red cedar, festooned with tylandria—the pines
    and cypresses, growing out of the white sand that
    spreads far and flat;
Rude boats descending the big Pedee—climbing
    plants, parasites, with coloured flowers and berries,
    enveloping huge trees,
The waving drapery on the live oak, trailing long and low,
    noiselessly waved by the wind;
The camp of Georgia waggoners, just after dark—the
    supper-fires, and the cooking and eating by whites
    and negroes,
Thirty or forty great waggons—the mules, cattle, horses,
    feeding from troughs,
The shadows, gleams, up under the leaves of the old
    sycamore-trees—the flames—also the black smoke
    from the pitch-pine, curling and rising;
Southern fishermen fishing—the sounds and inlets
    of North Carolina's coast—the shad-fishery and
    the herring-fishery—the large sweep- seines—the
    windlasses on shore worked by horses—the clearing,
    curing, and packing houses;
Deep in the forest, in piney woods, turpentine dropping
    from the incisions in the trees—There are the
    turpentine works,
There are the negroes at work, in good health—the
    ground in all directions is covered with pine straw.
—In Tennessee and Kentucky, slaves busy in the coalings,
    at the forge, by the furnace-blaze, or at the corn-
    shucking;
In Virginia, the planter's son returning after a long
    absence, joyfully welcomed and kissed by the aged
    mulatto nurse.

On rivers, boatmen safely moored at nightfall, in their
     boats, under shelter of high banks,
Some of the younger men dance to the sound of the banjo
     or fiddle—others sit on the gunwale, smoking and
     talking;
Late in the afternoon the mocking-bird, the American
     mimic, singing in the Great Dismal Swamp-there are
     the greenish waters, the resinous odour, the plenteous
     moss, the cypress-tree, and the juniper-tree.
—Northward, young men of Mannahatta—the target
     company from an excursion returning home at
     evening—the musket-muzzles all bear bunches of
     flowers presented by women;
Children at play—or on his father's lap a young boy fallen
     asleep, (how his lips move! how he smiles in his sleep!)
The scout riding on horseback over the plains west of the
     Mississippi—he ascends a knoll and sweeps his eye
     around.
California life—the miner, bearded, dressed in his rude
     costume—the staunch California friendship—the
     sweet air—the graves one, in passing, meets, solitary,
     just aside the horse-path;
Down in Texas, the cotton-field, the negro-cabins—
     drivers driving mules or oxen before rude carts—
     cotton-bales piled on banks and wharves.
Encircling all, vast-darting, up and wide, the American
     Soul, with equal hemispheres—one Love, one Dilation
     or Pride.
—In arriere, the peace-talk with the Iroquois, the
     aborigines—the calumet, the pipe of good-will,
     arbitration, and endorsement,
The sachem blowing the smoke first toward the sun and
     then toward the earth,
The drama of the scalp-dance enacted with painted faces
     and guttural exclamations,

The setting-out of the war-party—the long and stealthy
  march,
The single-file—the swinging hatchets—the surprise and
  slaughter of enemies.
—All the acts, scenes, ways, persons, attitudes, of these
  States— reminiscences, all institutions,
 All these States, compact—Every square mile of these
  States, without excepting a particle—you also—me
  also.
Me pleased, rambling in lanes and country fields,
  Paumanok's fields,
Me, observing the spiral flight of two little yellow
  butterflies, shuffling between each other, ascending
  high in the air;
The darting swallow, the destroyer of insects—the fall-
  traveller southward, but returning northward early in
  the spring;
The country boy at the close of the day, driving the herd
  of cows, and shouting to them as they loiter to browse
  by the roadside;
The city wharf—Boston, Philadelphia, Baltimore,
  Charleston, New Orleans, San Francisco,
The departing ships, when the sailors heave at the
  capstan;
Evening—me in my room—the setting sun,
The setting summer sun shining in my open window,
  showing the swarm of flies, suspended, balancing in
  the air in the centre of the room, darting athwart,
  up and down, casting swift shadows in specks on the
  opposite wall, where the shine is.
The athletic American matron speaking in public to
  crowds of listeners;
Males, females, immigrants, combinations—the
  copiousness—the individuality of the States, each for
  itself—the money-makers;

Factories, machinery, the mechanical forces—the
    windlass, lever, pulley— All certainties,
The certainty of space, increase, freedom, futurity;
In space, the sporades, the scattered islands, the stars—on
    the firm earth, the lands, my lands!
O lands! O all so dear to me—what you are (whatever it
    is), I become a part of that, whatever it is.
Southward there, I screaming, with wings slow-flapping,
    with the myriads of gulls wintering along the coasts
    of Florida—or in Louisiana, with pelicans breeding,
Otherways, there, atwixt the banks of the Arkansaw, the
    Rio Grande, the Nueces, the Brazos, the Tombigbee,
    the Red River, the Saskatchewan, or the Osage, I with
    the spring waters laughing and skipping and running;
Northward, on the sands, on some shallow bay of
    Paumanok, I, with parties of snowy herons wading in
    the wet to seek worms and aquatic plants;
Retreating, triumphantly twittering, the king-bird, from
    piercing the crow with its bill, for amusement—And I
    triumphantly twittering;
The migrating flock of wild geese alighting in autumn
    to refresh themselves—the body of the flock feed—
    the sentinels outside move around with erect heads
    watching, and are from time to time relieved by other
    sentinels—And I feeding and taking turns with the
    rest;
In Canadian forests, the moose, large as an ox, cornered
    by hunters, rising desperately on his hind-feet, and
    plunging with his fore-feet, the hoofs as sharp as
    knives—And I plunging at the hunters, cornered and
    desperate;
In the Mannahatta, streets, piers, shipping, store-houses,
    and the countless workmen working in the shops,

And I too of the Mannahatta, singing thereof—and no
   less in myself than the whole of the Mannahatta in
   itself,
Singing the song of These, my ever-united lands—my
   body no more inevitably united part to part, and
   made one identity, any more than my lands are
   inevitably united, and made ONE IDENTITY;
Nativities, climates, the grass of the great pastoral plains,
Cities, labours, death, animals, products, good and evil—
   these me,—
These affording, in all their particulars, endless feuillage
   to me and to America, how can I do less than pass the
   clue of the union of them, to afford the like to you?
Whoever you are! how can I but offer you divine leaves,
   that you also be eligible as I am?
How can I but, as here, chanting, invite you for yourself to
   collect bouquets of the incomparable feuillage of these
   States?

FOOTNOTES:

1. 1858-59.

THE PAST-PRESENT.

I was looking a long while for the history of the past for
    myself, and for these chants—and now I have found it.
It is not in those paged fables in the libraries, (them I
    neither accept nor reject;)
It is no more in the legends than in all else;
It is in the present—it is this earth to-day;
It is in Democracy—in this America—the Old World also;
It is the life of one man or one woman to-day, the average
    man of to-day;
It is languages, social customs, literatures, arts;
It is the broad show of artificial things, ships, machinery,
    politics, creeds, modern improvements, and the
    interchange of nations,
All for the average man of to-day.

YEARS OF THE UNPERFORMED.

Years of the unperformed! your horizon rises—I see it
    part away for more august dramas;
I see not America only—I see not only Liberty's nation but
    other nations embattling;
I see tremendous entrances and exits—I see new
    combinations—I see the solidarity of races;
I see that force advancing with irresistible power on the
    world's stage;
Have the old forces played their parts? are the acts suitable
    to them closed?
I see Freedom, completely armed, and victorious, and
    very haughty, with Law by her side, both issuing forth
    against the idea of caste;
—What historic denouements are these we so rapidly
    approach?
I see men marching and countermarching by swift
    millions!
I see the frontiers and boundaries of the old aristocracies
    broken;
I see the landmarks of European kings removed;
I see this day the People beginning their landmarks, all
    others give way;
Never were such sharp questions asked as this day;
Never was average man, his soul, more energetic, more
    like a God.
Lo! how he urges and urges, leaving the masses no rest;
His daring foot is on land and sea everywhere—he
    colonises the Pacific, the archipelagoes;

With the steam-ship, the electric telegraph, the
    newspaper, the wholesale engines of war,
With these, and the world-spreading factories, he
    interlinks all geography, all lands;
—What whispers are these, O lands, running ahead of
    you, passing under the
seas?
Are all nations communing? is there going to be but one
    heart to the globe?
Is humanity forming *en masse*?—for lo! tyrants tremble,
    crowns grow dim;
The earth, restive, confronts a new era, perhaps a general
    divine war;
No one knows what will happen next—such portents fill
    the days and nights.
Years prophetical! the space ahead as I walk, as I vainly
    try to pierce it, is full of phantoms;
Unborn deeds, things soon to be, project their shapes
    around me;
This incredible rush and heat—this strange ecstatic fever
    of dreams, O years!
Your dreams, O years, how they penetrate through me! (I
    know not whether I sleep or wake!)
The performed America and Europe grow dim, retiring in
    shadow behind me,
The unperformed, more gigantic than ever, advance,
    advance upon me.

FLUX.

Of these years I sing,
How they pass through convulsed pains, as through
    parturitions;
How America illustrates birth, gigantic youth, the
    promise, the sure fulfilment, despite of people—
    Illustrates evil as well as good;
How many hold despairingly yet to the models departed,
    caste, myths, obedience, compulsion, and to infidelity;
How few see the arrived models, the athletes, the States—
    or see freedom or spirituality—or hold any faith in
    results.
But I see the athletes—and I see the results glorious and
    inevitable—and they again leading to other results;
How the great cities appear—How the Democratic
    masses, turbulent, wilful, as I love them,
How the whirl, the contest, the wrestle of evil with good,
    the sounding and resounding, keep on and on;
How society waits unformed, and is between things
    ended and things begun;
How America is the continent of glories, and of the
    triumph of freedom, and of the Democracies, and of
    the fruits of society, and of all that is begun;
And how the States are complete in themselves—And how
    all triumphs and glories are complete in themselves,
    to lead onward,
And how these of mine, and of the States, will in their
    turn be convulsed, and serve other parturitions and
    transitions.

And how all people, sights, combinations, the Democratic
    masses, too, serve—and how every fact serves,
And how now, or at any time, each serves the exquisite
    transition of Death.

TO WORKING MEN.

1.

Come closer to me;
Push close, my lovers, and take the best I possess;
Yield closer and closer, and give me the best you possess.

This is unfinished business with me—How is it with you?
(I was chilled with the cold types, cylinder, wet paper
    between us.)

Male and Female!
I pass so poorly with paper and types, I must pass with
    the contact of bodies and souls.

American masses!
I do not thank you for liking me as I am, and liking the
    touch of me—I know that it is good for you to do so.

2.

This is the poem of occupations;
In the labour of engines and trades, and the labour of
    fields, I find the developments,
And find the eternal meanings.

Workmen and Workwomen!
Were all educations, practical and ornamental, well
    displayed out of me, what would it amount to?

Were I as the head teacher, charitable proprietor, wise
    statesman, what would it amount to?
Were I to you as the boss employing and paying you,
    would that satisfy you?

The learned, virtuous, benevolent, and the usual terms;
A man like me, and never the usual terms.

Neither a servant nor a master am I;
I take no sooner a large price than a small price—I will
    have my own, whoever enjoys me;
I will be even with you, and you shall be even with me.

If you stand at work in a shop, I stand as nigh as the
    nighest in the same shop;
If you bestow gifts on your brother or dearest friend, I
    demand as good as your brother or dearest friend;
If your lover, husband, wife, is welcome by day or night, I
    must be personally as welcome;
If you become degraded, criminal, ill, then I become so
    for your sake;
If you remember your foolish and outlawed deeds, do
    you think I cannot remember my own foolish and
    outlawed deeds?
If you carouse at the table, I carouse at the opposite side of
    the table;
 If you meet some stranger in the streets, and love him or
    her—why I often meet strangers in the street, and love
    them.

Why, what have you thought of yourself?
Is it you then that thought yourself less?
Is it you that thought the President greater than you?
Or the rich better off than you? or the educated wiser
    than you?

Because you are greasy or pimpled, or that you was once
    drunk, or a thief,
Or diseased, or rheumatic, or a prostitute, or are so now;
Or from frivolity or impotence, or that you are no scholar,
    and never saw your name in print,
Do you give in that you are any less immortal?

3.

Souls of men and women! it is not you I call unseen,
    unheard, untouchable and untouching;
It is not you I go argue pro and con about, and to settle
    whether you are alive or no;
I own publicly who you are, if nobody else owns.

Grown, half-grown, and babe, of this country and every
    country, indoors and outdoors, one just as much as
    the other, I see, And all else behind or through them.

The wife—and she is not one jot less than the husband;
The daughter—and she is just as good as the son;
The mother—and she is every bit as much as the father.

Offspring of ignorant and poor, boys apprenticed to
    trades,
Young fellows working on farms, and old fellows working
    on farms,
Sailor-men, merchant-men, coasters, immigrants,
All these I see—but nigher and farther the same I see;
None shall escape me, and none shall wish to escape me.

I bring what you much need, yet always have,
Not money, amours, dress, eating, but as good;

I send no agent or medium, offer no representative of
    value, but offer the value itself.

There is something that comes home to one now and
    perpetually;
It is not what is printed, preached, discussed—it eludes
    discussion and print;
It is not to be put in a book—it is not in this book;
It is for you, whoever you are—it is no farther from you
    than your hearing and sight are from you;
It is hinted by nearest, commonest, readiest—it is ever
    provoked by them.

You may read in many languages, yet read nothing about
    it;
You may read the President's Message, and read nothing
    about it there;
Nothing in the reports from the State department or
    Treasury department, or in the daily papers or the
    weekly papers,
Or in the census or revenue returns, prices current, or any
    accounts of stock.

4.

The sun and stars that float in the open air;
The apple-shaped earth, and we upon it—surely the drift
    of them is something grand!
I do not know what it is, except that it is grand, and that it
    is happiness,
And that the enclosing purport of us here is not a
    speculation, or bon-mot, or reconnoissance,
And that it is not something which by luck may turn out
    well for us, and without luck must be a failure for us,

And not something which may yet be retracted in a
    certain contingency.

The light and shade, the curious sense of body and
    identity, the greed that with perfect complaisance
    devours all things, the endless pride and outstretching
    of man, unspeakable joys and sorrows,
The wonder every one sees in every one else he sees, and
    the wonders that fill each minute of time for ever,
What have you reckoned them for, camerado?
Have you reckoned them for a trade, or farm-work? or for
    the profits of a store?
Or to achieve yourself a position? or to fill a gentleman's
    leisure, or a lady's leisure?

Have you reckoned the landscape took substance and
    form that it might be painted in a picture?
 Or men and women that they might be written of, and
    songs sung?
 Or the attraction of gravity, and the great laws and
    harmonious combinations, and the fluids of the air, as
    subjects for the savans?
Or the brown land and the blue sea for maps and charts?
Or the stars to be put in constellations and named fancy
    names?
Or that the growth of seeds is for agricultural tables, or
    agriculture itself?

Old institutions—these arts, libraries, legends, collections,
    and the practice handed along in manufactures—will
    we rate them so high?
Will we rate our cash and business high?—I have no
    objection;
I rate them as high as the highest—then a child born of a
    woman and man I rate beyond all rate.

We thought our Union grand, and our Constitution
    grand;
I do not say they are not grand and good, for they are;
I am this day just as much in love with them as you;
Then I am in love with you, and with all my fellows upon
    the earth.

We consider Bibles and religions divine—I do not say they
    are not divine;
I say they have all grown out of you, and may grow out of
    you still;
It is not they who give the life—it is you who give the life;
Leaves are not more shed from the trees, or trees from the
    earth, than they are shed out of you.

5.

When the psalm sings, instead of the singer;
When the script preaches, instead of the preacher;
When the pulpit descends and goes, instead of the carver
    that carved the supporting desk;
When I can touch the body of books, by night or by day,
    and when they touch my body back again;
When a university course convinces, like a slumbering
    woman and child convince;
When the minted gold in the vault smiles like the night-
    watchman's daughter;
When warrantee deeds loafe in chairs opposite, and are
    my friendly companions;
I intend to reach them my hand, and make as much of
    them as I do of men and women like you.

The sum of all known reverence I add up in you, whoever
    you are;

The President is there in the White House for you—it is
    not you who are here for him;
The Secretaries act in their bureaus for you—not you here
    for them;
The Congress convenes every twelfth month for you;
Laws, courts, the forming of States, the charters of cities,
    the going and coming of commerce and mails, are all
    for you.

List close, my scholars dear!
All doctrines, all politics and civilisation, exsurge from
    you;
All sculpture and monuments, and anything inscribed
    anywhere, are tallied in you;
The gist of histories and statistics, as far back as the
    records reach, is in you this hour, and myths and tales
    the same;
If you were not breathing and walking here, where would
    they all be?
The most renowned poems would be ashes, orations and
    plays would be vacuums.

All architecture is what you do to it when you look upon
    it;
Did you think it was in the white or grey stone? or the
    lines of the arches and cornices?

All music is what awakes from you, when you are
    reminded by the instruments;
It is not the violins and the cornets—it is not the oboe
    nor the beating drums, nor the score of the baritone
    singer singing his sweet romanza—nor that of the
    men's chorus, nor that of the women's chorus,
It is nearer and farther than they.

6.

Will the whole come back then?
Can each see signs of the best by a look in the looking-
    glass? is there nothing greater or more?
Does all sit there with you, with the mystic, unseen soul?

Strange and hard that paradox true I give;
Objects gross and the unseen Soul are one.

House-building, measuring, sawing the boards;
Blacksmithing, glass-blowing, nail-making, coopering,
    tin-roofing, shingle- dressing,
Ship-joining, dock-building, fish-curing, ferrying,
    flagging of side-walks by flaggers,
The pump, the pile-driver, the great derrick, the coal-kiln
    and brick-kiln,
Coal-mines, and all that is down there,—the lamps in the
    darkness, echoes, songs, what meditations, what vast
    native thoughts looking through smutched faces,
Ironworks, forge-fires in the mountains, or by the river-
    banks—men around feeling the melt with huge
    crowbars—lumps of ore, the due combining of ore,
    limestone, coal—the blast-furnace and the puddling-
    furnace, the loup-lump at the bottom of the melt at
    last— the rolling-mill, the stumpy bars of pig-iron, the
    strong, clean shaped T-rail for railroads;
Oilworks, silkworks, white-lead-works, the sugar-house,
    steam-saws, the great mills and factories;
Stone-cutting, shapely trimmings for façades, or window
    or door lintels— the mallet, the tooth-chisel, the jib to
    protect the thumb,
Oakum, the oakum-chisel, the caulking-iron—the kettle
    of boiling vault- cement, and the fire under the kettle,

The cotton-bale, the stevedore's hook, the saw and buck
of the sawyer, the mould of the moulder, the working
knife of the butcher, the ice- saw, and all the work
with ice,
The implements for daguerreotyping—the tools of the
rigger, grappler, sail-maker, block-maker,
Goods of gutta-percha, papier-mâché, colours, brushes,
brush-making, glaziers' implements,
The veneer and glue-pot, the confectioner's ornaments,
the decanter and glasses, the shears and flat-iron,
The awl and knee-strap, the pint measure and quart
measure, the counter and stool, the writing-pen of
quill or metal—the making of all sorts of edged tools,
The brewery, brewing, the malt, the vats, everything that
is done by brewers, also by wine-makers, also vinegar-
makers,
Leather-dressing, coach-making, boiler-making, rope-
twisting, distilling, sign-painting, lime-burning,
cotton-picking—electro-plating, electrotyping,
stereotyping,
Stave-machines, planing-machines, reaping-machines,
ploughing-machines, thrashing-machines, steam
waggons,
The cart of the carman, the omnibus, the ponderous dray;
Pyrotechny, letting off coloured fireworks at night, fancy
figures and jets,
Beef on the butcher's stall, the slaughter-house of the
butcher, the butcher in his killing-clothes,
The pens of live pork, the killing-hammer, the hog-hook,
the scalder's tub, gutting, the cutter's cleaver, the
packer's maul, and the plenteous winter-work of pork-
packing,
Flour-works, grinding of wheat, rye, maize, rice—the
barrels and the half and quarter barrels, the loaded
barges, the high piles on wharves and levees,

The men, and the work of the men, on railroads, coasters,
    fish-boats, canals;
The daily routine of your own or any man's life—the shop,
    yard, store, or factory;
These shows all near you by day and night-workmen!
    whoever you are, your daily life!
In that and them the heft of the heaviest—in them far
    more than you estimated, and far less also;
In them realities for you and me—in them poems for you
    and me;

In them, not yourself—you and your soul enclose all
    things, regardless of estimation;
In them the development good—in them, all themes and
    hints.

I do not affirm what you see beyond is futile—I do not
    advise you to stop;
I do not say leadings you thought great are not great;
But I say that none lead to greater than those lead to.

7.

Will you seek afar off? You surely come back at last,
In things best known to you finding the best, or as good
    as the best,
In folks nearest to you finding the sweetest, strongest,
    lovingest;
Happiness, knowledge, not in another place, but this
    place—not for another hour, but this hour;
Man in the first you see or touch—always in friend,
    brother, nighest neighbour—Woman in mother, sister,
    wife;
The popular tastes and employments taking precedence in
    poems or anywhere,

You workwomen and workmen of these States having
  your own divine and strong life,
And all else giving place to men and women like you.

SONG OF THE BROAD-AXE.

1.

Weapon, shapely, naked, wan; Head from the mother's
  bowels drawn!
Wooded flesh and metal bone! limb only one, and lip only
  one!
Grey-blue leaf by red-heat grown! helve produced from a
  little seed sown!
Resting the grass amid and upon,
To be leaned, and to lean on.

Strong shapes, and attributes of strong shapes—masculine
  trades, sights and sounds;
Long varied train of an emblem, dabs of music;
Fingers of the organist skipping staccato over the keys of
  the great organ.

2.

Welcome are all earth's lands, each for its kind;
Welcome are lands of pine and oak;
Welcome are lands of the lemon and fig;
Welcome are lands of gold;
Welcome are lands of wheat and maize—welcome those
  of the grape;
Welcome are lands of sugar and rice;
Welcome are cotton-lands—welcome those of the white
  potato and sweet potato;
Welcome are mountains, flats, sands, forests, prairies;

Welcome the rich borders of rivers, table-lands, openings,
Welcome the measureless grazing-lands—welcome the
    teeming soil of orchards, flax, honey, hemp;
Welcome just as much the other more hard-faced lands;
Lands rich as lands of gold, or wheat and fruit lands;
Lands of mines, lands of the manly and rugged ores;
Lands of coal, copper, lead, tin, zinc;
LANDS OF IRON! lands of the make of the axe!

3.

The log at the wood-pile, the axe supported by it;
The sylvan hut, the vine over the doorway, the space
    cleared for a garden,
The irregular tapping of rain down on the leaves, after the
    storm is lulled,
The wailing and moaning at intervals, the thought of the
    sea,
The thought of ships struck in the storm, and put on their
    beam-ends, and the cutting away of masts;
The sentiment of the huge timbers of old-fashioned
    houses and barns;
The remembered print or narrative, the voyage at a
    venture of men, families, goods,
The disembarkation, the founding of a new city,
The voyage of those who sought a New England and
    found it—the outset anywhere,
The settlements of the Arkansas, Colorado, Ottawa,
    Willamette,
The slow progress, the scant fare, the axe, rifle, saddle-
    bags;
The beauty of all adventurous and daring persons,
The beauty of wood-boys and wood-men, with their clear
    untrimmed faces,

The beauty of independence, departure, actions that rely
    on themselves,
The American contempt for statutes and ceremonies, the
    boundless impatience of restraint,
The loose drift of character, the inkling through random
    types, the solidification;
The butcher in the slaughter-house, the hands aboard
    schooners and sloops, the raftsman, the pioneer,
Lumbermen in their winter camp, daybreak in the woods,
    stripes of snow on the limbs of trees, the occasional
    snapping,
The glad clear sound of one's own voice, the merry song,
    the natural life of the woods, the strong day's work,
The blazing fire at night, the sweet taste of supper, the
    talk, the bed of hemlock boughs, and the bearskin;
—The house-builder at work in cities or anywhere,
The preparatory jointing, squaring, sawing, mortising,
The hoist-up of beams, the push of them in their places,
    laying them regular, Setting the studs by their tenons
    in the mortises, according as they were prepared,
The blows of mallets and hammers, the attitudes of the
    men, their curved limbs,
Bending, standing, astride the beams, driving in pins,
    holding on by posts and braces,
The hooked arm over the plate, the other arm wielding
    the axe,
The floor-men forcing the planks close, to be nailed,
Their postures bringing their weapons downward on the
    bearers,
The echoes resounding through the vacant building;
The huge store-house carried up in the city, well under
    way,
The six framing men, two in the middle, and two at each
    end, carefully bearing on their shoulders a heavy stick
    for a cross-beam,

The crowded line of masons with trowels in their right
    hands, rapidly laying the long side-wall, two hundred
    feet from front to rear,
The flexible rise and fall of backs, the continual click of
    the trowels striking the bricks,
The bricks, one after another, each laid so workmanlike in
    its place, and set with a knock of the trowel-handle,
The piles of materials, the mortar on the mortar-boards,
    and the steady replenishing by the hod-men;
—Spar-makers in the spar-yard, the swarming row of
    well-grown apprentices,
The swing of their axes on the square-hewed log, shaping
    it toward the shape of a mast,
The brisk short crackle of the steel driven slantingly into
    the pine,
The butter-coloured chips flying off in great flakes and
    slivers,
The limber motion of brawny young arms and hips in
    easy costumes;
The constructor of wharves, bridges, piers, bulk-heads,
    floats, stays against the sea;
—The city fireman—the fire that suddenly bursts forth in
    the close-packed square,
The arriving engines, the hoarse shouts, the nimble
    stepping and daring,
The strong command through the fire-trumpets, the
    falling in line, the rise and fall of the arms forcing the
    water,
The slender, spasmic blue-white jets—the bringing to bear
    of the hooks and ladders, and their execution,
The crash and cut-away of connecting woodwork, or
    through floors, if the fire smoulders under them,
The crowd with their lit faces, watching—the glare and
    dense shadows;

—The forger at his forge-furnace, and the user of iron
    after him,
The maker of the axe large and small, and the welder and
    temperer,
The chooser breathing his breath on the cold steel, and
    trying the edge with his thumb,
The one who clean-shapes the handle and sets it firmly in
    the socket;
The shadowy processions of the portraits of the past users
    also,
The primal patient mechanics, the architects and
    engineers,
The far-off Assyrian edifice and Mizra edifice,
The Roman lictors preceding the consuls,
The antique European warrior with his axe in combat,
The uplifted arm, the clatter of blows on the helmeted
    head,
The death-howl, the limpsey tumbling body, the rush of
    friend and foe thither,
The siege of revolted lieges determined for liberty,
The summons to surrender, the battering at castle-gates,
    the truce and parley;
The sack of an old city in its time,
The bursting in of mercenaries and bigots tumultuously
    and disorderly,
Roar, flames, blood, drunkenness, madness,
Goods freely rifled from houses and temples, screams of
    women in the gripe of brigands,
Craft and thievery of camp-followers, men running, old
    persons despairing,
The hell of war, the cruelties of creeds,
The list of all executive deeds and words, just or unjust,
The power of personality, just or unjust.

4.

Muscle and pluck for ever!
What invigorates life invigorates death,
And the dead advance as much as the living advance,
And the future is no more uncertain than the present,
And the roughness of the earth and of man encloses as
    much as the *delicatesse* of the earth and of man,
And nothing endures but personal qualities.

What do you think endures?
Do you think the great city endures?
Or a teeming manufacturing state? or a prepared
    constitution? or the best- built steamships?
Or hotels of granite and iron? or any *chefs-d'oeuvre* of
    engineering, forts, armaments?

Away! These are not to be cherished for themselves;
They fill their hour, the dancers dance, the musicians play
    for them;
The show passes, all does well enough of course,
All does very well till one flash of defiance.

The great city is that which has the greatest man or
    woman;
If it be a few ragged huts, it is still the greatest city in the
    whole world.

5.

The place where the great city stands is not the place of
    stretched wharves, docks, manufactures, deposits of
    produce,
Nor the place of ceaseless salutes of new-comers, or the
    anchor-lifters of the departing,

Nor the place of the tallest and costliest buildings, or
    shops selling goods from the rest of the earth,
Nor the place of the best libraries and schools—nor the
    place where money is plentiest,
Nor the place of the most numerous population.

Where the city stands with the brawniest breed of orators
    and bards;
Where the city stands that is beloved by these, and loves
    them in return, and understands them;
Where no monuments exist to heroes but in the common
    words and deeds;
Where thrift is in its place, and prudence is in its place;
Where the men and women think lightly of the laws;
Where the slave ceases, and the master of slaves ceases;
Where the populace rise at once against the never-ending
    audacity of elected persons;
Where fierce men and women pour forth, as the sea to
    the whistle of death pours its sweeping and unripped
    waves;
Where outside authority enters always after the
    precedence of inside authority;
Where the citizen is always the head and ideal—and
    President, Mayor, Governor, and what not, are agents
    for pay;
Where children are taught to be laws to themselves, and
    to depend on themselves;
Where equanimity is illustrated in affairs;
Where speculations on the Soul are encouraged;
Where women walk in public processions in the streets,
    the same as the men;
Where they enter the public assembly and take places the
    same as the men;
Where the city of the faithfullest friends stands;
Where the city of the cleanliness of the sexes stands;

Where the city of the healthiest fathers stands;
Where the city of the best-bodied mothers stands,—
There the great city stands.

6.

How beggarly appear arguments before a defiant deed!
How the floridness of the materials of cities shrivels
      before a man's or woman's look!

All waits, or goes by default, till a strong being appears;
A strong being is the proof of the race, and of the ability
      of the universe;
When he or she appears, materials are overawed,
The dispute on the Soul stops,
The old customs and phrases are confronted, turned back,
      or laid away.

What is your money-making now? What can it do now?
What is your respectability now?
What are your theology, tuition, society, traditions,
      statute-books, now?
Where are your jibes of being now?
Where are your cavils about the Soul now?

Was that your best? Were those your vast and solid?
Riches, opinions, politics, institutions, to part obediently
      from the path of one man or woman!
The centuries, and all authority, to be trod under the foot-
      soles of one man or woman!

7.

A sterile landscape covers the ore—there is as good as the
      best, for all the forbidding appearance;

There is the mine, there are the miners;
The forge-furnace is there, the melt is accomplished;
   the hammersmen are at hand with their tongs and
   hammers;
What always served and always serves is at hand.

Than this nothing has better served—it has served all:
Served the fluent-tongued and subtle-sensed Greek, and
   long ere the Greek;
Served in building the buildings that last longer than any;
Served the Hebrew, the Persian, the most ancient
   Hindostanee;
Served the mound-raiser on the Mississippi—served those
   whose relics remain in Central America;
Served Albic temples in woods or on plains, with unhewn
   pillars, and the druids;
Served the artificial clefts, vast, high, silent, on the snow-
   covered hills of Scandinavia;
Served those who, time out of mind, made on the granite
   walls rough sketches of the sun, moon, stars, ships,
   ocean-waves;
Served the paths of the irruptions of the Goths—served
   the pastoral tribes and nomads;
Served the long long distant Kelt—served the hardy
   pirates of the Baltic;
Served, before any of those, the venerable and harmless
   men of Ethiopia;
Served the making of helms for the galleys of pleasure,
   and the making of those for war;
Served all great works on land, and all great works on the
   sea;
For the mediaeval ages, and before the mediaeval ages;
Served not the living only, then as now, but served the
   dead.

8.

I see the European headsman;
He stands masked, clothed in red, with huge legs and
    strong naked arms,
And leans on a ponderous axe.

Whom have you slaughtered lately, European headsman?
Whose is that blood upon you, so wet and sticky?

I see the clear sunsets of the martyrs;
I see from the scaffolds the descending ghosts,
Ghosts of dead lords, uncrowned ladies, impeached
    ministers, rejected kings,
Rivals, traitors, poisoners, disgraced chieftains, and the
    rest.

I see those who in any land have died for the good cause;
The seed is spare, nevertheless the crop shall never run
    out;
(Mind you, O foreign kings, O priests, the crop shall
    never run out.)

I see the blood washed entirely away from the axe;
Both blade and helve are clean;
They spirt no more the blood of European nobles—they
    clasp no more the necks of queens.

I see the headsman withdraw and become useless;
I see the scaffold untrodden and mouldy—I see no longer
    any axe upon it;
I see the mighty and friendly emblem of the power of my
    own race—the newest, largest race.

9.

America! I do not vaunt my love for you;
I have what I have.

The axe leaps!
The solid forest gives fluid utterances;
They tumble forth, they rise and form,
Hut, tent, landing, survey,
Flail, plough, pick, crowbar, spade,
Shingle, rail, prop, wainscot, jamb, lath, panel, gable,
Citadel, ceiling, saloon, academy, organ, exhibition house,
    library,
Cornice, trellis, pilaster, balcony, window, shutter, turret,
    porch,
Hoe, rake, pitchfork, pencil, waggon, staff, saw, jack-plane,
    mallet, wedge, rounce,
Chair, tub, hoop, table, wicket, vane, sash, floor,
Work-box, chest, stringed instrument, boat, frame, and
    what not,
Capitols of States, and capitol of the nation of States,
Long stately rows in avenues, hospitals for orphans, or for
    the poor or sick,
Manhattan steamboats and clippers, taking the measure
    of all seas.

The shapes arise!
Shapes of the using of axes anyhow, and the users, and all
    that neighbours them,
Cutters-down of wood, and haulers of it to the Penobscot
    or Kennebec,
Dwellers in cabins among the Californian mountains, or
    by the little lakes, or on the Columbia,
Dwellers south on the banks of the Gila or Rio Grande—
    friendly gatherings, the characters and fun,

Dwellers up north in Minnesota and by the Yellowstone
　　river—dwellers on coasts and off coasts,
Seal-fishers, whalers, arctic seamen breaking passages
　　through the ice.

The shapes arise!
Shapes of factories, arsenals, foundries, markets;
Shapes of the two-threaded tracks of railroads;
Shapes of the sleepers of bridges, vast frameworks,
　　girders, arches;
Shapes of the fleets of barges, tows, lake craft, river craft.

The shapes arise!
Shipyards and dry-docks along the Eastern and Western
　　Seas, and in many a bay and by-place,
The live-oak kelsons, the pine-planks, the spars, the
　　hackmatack-roots for knees,
The ships themselves on their ways, the tiers of scaffolds,
　　the workmen busy outside and inside,
The tools lying around, the great auger and little auger,
　　the adze, bolt, line, square, gouge, and bead-plane.

10.

The shapes arise!
The shape measured, sawed, jacked, joined, stained,
The coffin-shape for the dead to lie within in his shroud;
The shape got out in posts, in the bedstead posts, in the
　　posts of the bride's bed;
The shape of the little trough, the shape of the rockers
　　beneath, the shape of the babe's cradle;
The shape of the floor-planks, the floor-planks for
　　dancers' feet;
The shape of the planks of the family home, the home of
　　the friendly parents and children,

The shape of the roof of the home of the happy young
    man and woman, the roof over the well-married
    young man and woman,
The roof over the supper joyously cooked by the chaste
    wife, and joyously eaten by the chaste husband,
    content after his day's work.

The shapes arise!
The shape of the prisoner's place in the court-room, and of
    him or her seated in the place;
The shape of the liquor-bar leaned against by the young
    rum-drinker and the old rum-drinker;
The shape of the shamed and angry stairs, trod, by
    sneaking footsteps;
The shape of the sly settee, and the adulterous
    unwholesome couple;
The shape of the gambling-board with its devilish
    winnings and losings;
The shape of the step-ladder for the convicted and
    sentenced murderer, the murderer with haggard face
    and pinioned arms,
The sheriff at hand with his deputies, the silent and white-
    lipped crowd, the sickening dangling of the rope.

The shapes arise!
Shapes of doors giving many exits and entrances;
The door passing the dissevered friend, flushed and in
    haste;
The door that admits good news and bad news;
The door whence the son left home, confident and puffed
    up;
The door he entered again from a long and scandalous
    absence, diseased, broken down, without innocence,
    without means.

11.

Her shape arises,
She less guarded than ever, yet more guarded than ever;
The gross and soiled she moves among do not make her
    gross and soiled;
She knows the thoughts as she passes—nothing is
    concealed from her;
She is none the less considerate or friendly therefor;
She is the best beloved—it is without exception—she has
    no reason to fear, and she does not fear;
Oaths, quarrels, hiccupped songs, smutty expressions, are
    idle to her as she passes;
She is silent—she is possessed of herself—they do not
    offend her;
She receives them as the laws of nature receive them—she
    is strong,
She too is a law of nature—there is no law stronger than
    she is.

12.

The main shapes arise!
Shapes of Democracy, total result of centuries;
Shapes, ever projecting other shapes;
Shapes of a hundred Free States, begetting another
    hundred;
Shapes of turbulent manly cities;
Shapes of the women fit for these States,
Shapes of the friends and home-givers of the whole earth,
Shapes bracing the earth, and braced with the whole
    earth.

ANTECEDENTS.

1.

With antecedents;
With my fathers and mothers, and the accumulations of
    past ages:
With all which, had it not been, I would not now be here,
    as I am;
With Egypt, India, Phoenicia, Greece, and Rome;
With the Kelt, the Scandinavian, the Alb, and the Saxon;
With antique maritime ventures,—with laws, artisanship,
    wars, and journeys;
With the poet, the skald, the saga, the myth, and the
    oracle;
With the sale of slaves—with enthusiasts—with the
    troubadour, the crusader, and the monk;
With those old continents whence we have come to this
    new continent;
With the fading kingdoms and kings over there;
With the fading religions and priests;
With the small shores we look back to from our own large
    and present shores;
With countless years drawing themselves onward, and
    arrived at these years;
You and Me arrived—America arrived, and making this
    year;
This year! sending itself ahead countless years to come.

2.

O but it is not the years—it is I—it is You;
We touch all laws, and tally all antecedents;
We are the skald, the oracle, the monk, and the knight—
    we easily include them, and more;
We stand amid time, beginningless and endless—we
    stand amid evil and good;
All swings around us—there is as much darkness as light;
The very sun swings itself and its system of planets
    around us:
Its sun, and its again, all swing around us.

3.

As for me, (torn, stormy, even as I, amid these vehement
    days;)
I have the idea of all, and am all, and believe in all;
I believe materialism is true, and spiritualism is true—I
    reject no part.

Have I forgotten any part?
Come to me, whoever and whatever, till I give you
    recognition.

I respect Assyria, China, Teutonia, and the Hebrews;
I adopt each theory, myth, god, and demi-god;
I see that the old accounts, bibles, genealogies, are true,
    without exception;
I assert that all past days were what they should have
    been;
And that they could nohow have been better than they
    were,
And that to-day is what it should be—and that America
    is,

And that to-day and America could nohow be better than
they are.

4.

In the name of these States, and in your and my name, the
Past,
And in the name of these States, and in your and my
name, the Present time.

I know that the past was great, and the future will be
great,
And I know that both curiously conjoint in the present
time,
For the sake of him I typify—for the common average
man's sake—your sake, if you are he;
And that where I am, or you are, this present day, there is
the centre of all days, all races,
And there is the meaning, to us, of all that has ever come
of races and days, or ever will come.

SALUT AU MONDE!

1.

O take my hand, Walt Whitman!
Such gliding wonders! such sights and sounds!
Such joined unended links, each hooked to the next!
Each answering all—each sharing the earth with all.

What widens within you, Walt Whitman?
What waves and soils exuding?
What climes? what persons and lands are here?
Who are the infants? some playing, some slumbering?
Who are the girls? who are the married women?
Who are the three old men going slowly with their arms
    about each others' necks?
What rivers are these? what forests and fruits are these?
What are the mountains called that rise so high in the
    mists?
What myriads of dwellings are they, filled with dwellers?

2.

Within me latitude widens, longitude lengthens;
Asia, Africa, Europe, are to the east—America is provided
    for in the west;
Banding the bulge of the earth winds the hot equator,
Curiously north and south turn the axis-ends;
Within me is the longest day—the sun wheels in slanting
    rings—it does not set for months.

Stretched in due time within me the midnight sun just
    rises above the horizon, and sinks again;
Within me zones, seas, cataracts, plants, volcanoes,
    groups,
Malaysia, Polynesia, and the great West Indian islands.

3.

What do you hear, Walt Whitman?

I hear the workman singing, and the farmer's wife
    singing;
I hear in the distance the sounds of children, and of
    animals early in the day;
I hear quick rifle-cracks from the riflemen of East
    Tennessee and Kentucky, hunting on hills;
I hear emulous shouts of Australians, pursuing the wild
    horse;
I hear the Spanish dance, with castanets, in the chestnut
    shade, to the rebeck and guitar;
I hear continual echoes from the Thames;
I hear fierce French liberty songs;
I hear of the Italian boat-sculler the musical recitative of
    old poems;
I hear the Virginian plantation chorus of negroes, of a
    harvest night, in the glare of pine-knots;
I hear the strong barytone of the 'long-shore-men of
    Mannahatta;
I hear the stevedores unlading the cargoes, and singing;
I hear the screams of the water-fowl of solitary north-west
    lakes;
I hear the rustling pattering of locusts, as they strike the
    grain and grass with the showers of their terrible
    clouds;

121

I hear the Coptic refrain, toward sundown, pensively
    falling on the breast of the black venerable vast
    mother, the Nile;
I hear the bugles of raft-tenders on the streams of Canada;
I hear the chirp of the Mexican muleteer, and the bells of
    the mule;
I hear the Arab muezzin, calling from the top of the
    mosque;
I hear the Christian priests at the altars of their
    churches—I hear the responsive bass and soprano;
I hear the wail of utter despair of the white-haired Irish
    grandparents, when they learn the death of their
    grandson;
I hear the cry of the Cossack, and the sailor's voice,
    putting to sea at Okotsk;
I hear the wheeze of the slave-coffle, as the slaves march
    on—as the husky gangs pass on by twos and threes,
    fastened together with wrist- chains and ankle-chains;
I hear the entreaties of women tied up for punishment—I
    hear the sibilant whisk of thongs through the air;
I hear the Hebrew reading his records and psalms;
I hear the rhythmic myths of the Greeks, and the strong
    legends of the Romans;
I hear the tale of the divine life and bloody death of the
    beautiful God, the Christ;
I hear the Hindoo teaching his favourite pupil the loves,
    wars, adages, transmitted safely to this day from poets
    who wrote three thousand years ago.

4.

What do you see, Walt Whitman?
Who are they you salute, and that one after another salute
    you?

I see a great round wonder rolling through the air:
I see diminute farms, hamlets, ruins, grave-yards, jails,
    factories, palaces, hovels, huts of barbarians, tents of
    nomads, upon the surface;
I see the shaded part on one side, where the sleepers are
    sleeping—and the sun-lit part on the other side;
I see the curious silent change of the light and shade;
I see distant lands, as real and near to the inhabitants of
    them as my land is to me.

I see plenteous waters;
I see mountain-peaks—I see the sierras of Andes and
    Alleghanies, where they range;
I see plainly the Himalayas, Chian Shahs, Altays, Ghauts;
I see the Rocky Mountains, and the Peak of Winds;
I see the Styrian Alps, and the Karnac Alps;
I see the Pyrenees, Balks, Carpathians—and to the north
    the Dofrafields, and off at sea Mount Hecla;
I see Vesuvius and Etna—I see the Anahuacs;
I see the Mountains of the Moon, and the Snow
    Mountains, and the Red Mountains of Madagascar;
I see the Vermont hills, and the long string of Cordilleras;
I see the vast deserts of Western America;
I see the Libyan, Arabian, and Asiatic deserts;
I see huge dreadful Arctic and Anarctic icebergs;
I see the superior oceans and the inferior ones—the
    Atlantic and Pacific, the sea of Mexico, the Brazilian
    sea, and the sea of Peru,
The Japan waters, those of Hindostan, the China Sea, and
    the Gulf of Guinea,
The spread of the Baltic, Caspian, Bothnia, the British
    shores, and the Bay of Biscay,
The clear-sunned Mediterranean, and from one to
    another of its islands,
The inland fresh-tasted seas of North America,

The White Sea, and the sea around Greenland.

I behold the mariners of the world;
Some are in storms—some in the night, with the watch on
the look-out;
Some drifting helplessly—some with contagious diseases.

I behold the sail and steam ships of the world, some in
clusters in port, some on their voyages;
Some double the Cape of Storms—some Cape Verde,—
others Cape Guardafui, Bon, or Bajadore;
Others Dondra Head—others pass the Straits of Sunda—
others Cape Lopatka— others Behring's Straits;
Others Cape Horn—others the Gulf of Mexico, or along
Cuba or Hayti—others Hudson's Bay or Baffin's Bay;
Others pass the Straits of Dover—others enter the
Wash—others the Firth of Solway—others round
Cape Clear—others the Land's End;
Others traverse the Zuyder Zee, or the Scheld;
Others add to the exits and entrances at Sandy Hook;
Others to the comers and goers at Gibraltar, or the
Dardanelles;
Others sternly push their way through the northern
winter-packs;
Others descend or ascend the Obi or the Lena:
Others the Niger or the Congo—others the Indus, the
Burampooter and Cambodia;
Others wait at the wharves of Manhattan, steamed up,
ready to start;
Wait, swift and swarthy, in the ports of Australia;
Wait at Liverpool, Glasgow, Dublin, Marseilles, Lisbon,
Naples, Hamburg, Bremen, Bordeaux, the Hague,
Copenhagen;
Wait at Valparaiso, Rio Janeiro, Panama;

Wait at their moorings at Boston, Philadelphia, Baltimore,
  Charleston, New Orleans, Galveston, San Francisco.

5.

I see the tracks of the railroads of the earth;
I see them welding State to State, city to city, through
  North America;
I see them in Great Britain, I see them in Europe;
I see them in Asia and in Africa.

I see the electric telegraphs of the earth; I see the
  filaments of the news of the wars, deaths, losses, gains,
  passions, of my race.
I see the long river-stripes of the earth;
I see where the Mississippi flows—I see where the
  Columbia flows;
I see the Great River, and the Falls of Niagara;
I see the Amazon and the Paraguay;
I see the four great rivers of China, the Amour, the Yellow
  River, the Yiang-tse, and the Pearl;
I see where the Seine flows, and where the Loire, the
  Rhone, and the Guadalquivir flow;
I see the windings of the Volga, the Dnieper, the Oder;
I see the Tuscan going down the Arno, and the Venetian
  along the Po;
I see the Greek seaman sailing out of Egina bay.

6.

I see the site of the old empire of Assyria, and that of
  Persia, and that of India;
I see the falling of the Ganges over the high rim of
  Saukara.

125

I see the place of the idea of the Deity incarnated by
    avatars in human forms;
I see the spots of the successions of priests on the earth—
    oracles, sacrificers, brahmins, sabians, lamas, monks,
    muftis, exhorters;
I see where druids walked the groves of Mona—I see the
    mistletoe and vervain;
I see the temples of the deaths of the bodies of Gods—I
    see the old signifiers.

I see Christ once more eating the bread of His last supper,
    in the midst of youths and old persons:
I see where the strong divine young man, the Hercules,
    toiled faithfully and long, and then died;
I see the place of the innocent rich life and hapless fate of
    the beautiful nocturnal son, the full-limbed Bacchus;
I see Kneph, blooming, drest in blue, with the crown of
    feathers on his head;
I see Hermes, unsuspected, dying, well-beloved, saying to
    the people, *Do not weep for me,*
This is not my true country, I have lived banished from my
    true country—I now go back there,
I return to the celestial sphere, where every one goes in his
    turn.

7.

I see the battlefields of the earth—grass grows upon them,
    and blossoms and corn;
I see the tracks of ancient and modern expeditions.

I see the nameless masonries, venerable messages of the
    unknown events, heroes, records of the earth;
I see the places of the sagas;
I see pine-trees and fir-frees torn by northern blasts;

126

I see granite boulders and cliffs—I see green meadows
    and lakes;
I see the burial-cairns of Scandinavian warriors;
I see them raised high with stones, by the marge of
    restless oceans, that the dead men's spirits, when they
    wearied of their quiet graves, might rise up through
    the mounds, and gaze on the tossing billows, and be
    refreshed by storms, immensity, liberty, action.

I see the steppes of Asia;
I see the tumuli of Mongolia—I see the tents of Kalmucks
    and Baskirs;
I see the nomadic tribes, with herds of oxen and cows;
I see the table-lands notched with ravines—I see the
    jungles and deserts;
I see the camel, the wild steed, the bustard, the fat-tailed
    sheep, the antelope, and the burrowing-wolf.

I see the highlands of Abyssinia;
I see flocks of goats feeding, and see the fig-tree,
    tamarind, date,
And see fields of teff-wheat, and see the places of verdure
    and gold.

I see the Brazilian vaquero;
I see the Bolivian ascending Mount Sorata;
I see the Wacho crossing the plains—I see the
    incomparable rider of horses
with his lasso on his arm;
I see over the pampas the pursuit of wild cattle for their
    hides.

8.

I see little and large sea-dots, some inhabited, some
    uninhabited; I see two boats with nets, lying off the
    shore of Paumanok, quite still;
I see ten fishermen waiting—they discover now a thick
    school of mossbonkers—they drop the joined sein-
    ends in the water,
The boats separate—they diverge and row off, each
    on its rounding course to the beach, enclosing the
    mossbonkers;
The net is drawn in by a windlass by those who stop
    ashore,
Some of the fishermen lounge in their boats—others
    stand negligently ankle-deep in the water, poised on
    strong legs;
The boats are partly drawn up—the water slaps against
    them;
On the sand, in heaps and winrows, well out from the
    water, lie the green- backed spotted mossbonkers.

9.

I see the despondent red man in the west, lingering about
    the banks of Moingo, and about Lake Pepin;
He has heard the quail and beheld the honey-bee, and
    sadly prepared to depart.

I see the regions of snow and ice;
I see the sharp-eyed Samoiede and the Finn;
I see the seal-seeker in his boat, poising his lance;
I see the Siberian on his slight-built sledge, drawn by
    dogs;
I see the porpess-hunters—I see the whale-crews of the
    South Pacific and the North Atlantic;

I see the cliffs, glaciers, torrents, valleys, of Switzerland—I
    mark the long winters, and the isolation.

I see the cities of the earth, and make myself at random a
    part of them;
I am a real Parisian;
I am a habitant of Vienna, St. Petersburg, Berlin,
    Constantinople;
I am of Adelaide, Sidney, Melbourne;
I am of London, Manchester, Bristol, Edinburgh,
    Limerick,
I am of Madrid, Cadiz, Barcelona, Oporto, Lyons,
    Brussels, Berne, Frankfort, Stuttgart, Turin, Florence;
I belong in Moscow, Cracow, Warsaw—or northward in
    Christiania or Stockholm—or in Siberian Irkutsk—or
    in some street in Iceland;
I descend upon all those cities, and rise from them again.

10.

I see vapours exhaling from unexplored countries;
I see the savage types, the bow and arrow, the poisoned
    splint, the fetish, and the obi.

I see African and Asiatic towns;
I see Algiers, Tripoli, Derne, Mogadore, Timbuctoo,
    Monrovia;
I see the swarms of Pekin, Canton, Benares, Delhi,
    Calcutta, Yedo;
I see the Kruman in his hut, and the Dahoman and
    Ashantee-man in their huts;
I see the Turk smoking opium in Aleppo;
I see the picturesque crowds at the fairs of Khiva, and
    those of Herat;

I see Teheran—I see Muscat and Medina, and the
    intervening sands—I see the caravans toiling onward;
I see Egypt and the Egyptians—I see the pyramids and
    obelisks;
I look on chiselled histories, songs, philosophies, cut in
    slabs of sandstone or on granite blocks;
I see at Memphis mummy-pits, containing mummies,
    embalmed, swathed in linen cloth, lying there many
    centuries;
I look on the fallen Theban, the large-balled eyes, the side-
    drooping neck, the hands folded across the breast.

I see the menials of the earth, labouring;
I see the prisoners in the prisons;
I see the defective human bodies of the earth;
I see the blind, the deaf and dumb, idiots, hunchbacks,
    lunatics;
I see the pirates, thieves, betrayers, murderers, slave-
    makers of the earth;
I see the helpless infants, and the helpless old men and
    women.

I see male and female everywhere;
I see the serene brotherhood of philosophs;
I see the constructiveness of my race;
I see the results of the perseverance and industry of my
    race;
I see ranks, colours, barbarisms, civilisations—I go
    among them—I mix indiscriminately,
And I salute all the inhabitants of the earth.

11.

You, where you are!
You daughter or son of England!

You of the mighty Slavic tribes and empires! you Russ in
    Russia!
You dim-descended, black, divine-souled African, large,
    fine-headed, nobly-formed, superbly destined, on
    equal terms with me!
You Norwegian! Swede! Dane! Icelander! you Prussian!
You Spaniard of Spain! you Portuguese!
You Frenchwoman and Frenchman of France!
You Belge! you liberty-lover of the Netherlands!
You sturdy Austrian! you Lombard! Hun! Bohemian!
    farmer of Styria!
You neighbour of the Danube!
You working-man of the Rhine, the Elbe, or the Weser!
    you working-woman too!
You Sardinian! you Bavarian! Swabian! Saxon!
    Wallachian! Bulgarian!
You citizen of Prague! Roman! Neapolitan! Greek!
You lithe matador in the arena at Seville!
You mountaineer living lawlessly on the Taurus or
    Caucasus!
You Bokh horse-herd, watching your mares and stallions
    feeding!
You beautiful-bodied Persian, at full speed in the saddle
    shooting arrows to the mark!
You Chinaman and Chinawoman of China! you Tartar of
    Tartary!
You women of the earth subordinated at your tasks!
You Jew journeying in your old age through every risk, to
    stand once on Syrian ground!
You other Jews waiting in all lands for your Messiah!
You thoughtful Armenian, pondering by some stream
    of the Euphrates! you peering amid the ruins of
    Nineveh! you ascending Mount Ararat!
You foot-worn pilgrim welcoming the far-away sparkle of
    the minarets of Mecca!

You sheiks along the stretch from Suez to Babelmandeb,
     ruling your families and tribes!
You olive-grower tending your fruit on fields of Nazareth,
     Damascus, or Lake Tiberias!
You Thibet trader on the wide inland, or bargaining in
     the shops of Lassa!
You Japanese man or woman! you liver in Madagascar,
     Ceylon, Sumatra, Borneo!
All you continentals of Asia, Africa, Europe, Australia,
     indifferent of place!
All you on the numberless islands of the archipelagoes of
     the sea!
And you of centuries hence, when you listen to me!
And you, each and everywhere, whom I specify not, but
     include just the same!
Health to you! Goodwill to you all—from me and
     America sent.

Each of us inevitable;
Each of us limitless—each of us with his or her right upon
     the earth;
Each of us allowed the eternal purports of the earth:
Each of us here as divinely as any is here.

12.

You Hottentot with clicking palate! You woolly-haired
     hordes!
You owned persons, dropping sweat-drops or blood-
     drops!
You human forms with the fathomless ever-impressive
     countenances of brutes!
I dare not refuse you—the scope of the world, and of time
     and space, are upon me.

You poor koboo whom the meanest of the rest look
    down upon, for all your glimmering language and
    spirituality!
You low expiring aborigines of the hills of Utah, Oregon,
    California!
You dwarfed Kamtschatkan, Greenlander, Lap!
You Austral negro, naked, red, sooty, with protrusive lip,
    grovelling, seeking your food!
You Caffre, Berber, Soudanese!
You haggard, uncouth, untutored Bedowee!
You plague-swarms in Madras, Nankin, Kaubul, Cairo!
You bather bathing in the Ganges!
You benighted roamer of Amazonia! you Patagonian! you
    Fejee-man!
You peon of Mexico! you slave of Carolina, Texas,
    Tennessee!
I do not prefer others so very much before you either;
I do not say one word against you, away back there, where
    you stand;
You will come forward in due time to my side.

My spirit has passed in compassion and determination
    around the whole earth;
I have looked for equals and lovers, and found them ready
    for me in all lands;
I think some divine rapport has equalised me with them.

13.

O vapours! I think I have risen with you, and moved
    away to distant continents, and fallen down there, for
    reasons;
I think I have blown with you, O winds;
O waters, I have fingered every shore with you.

I have run through what any river or strait of the globe
    has run through;
I have taken my stand on the bases of peninsulas, and on
    the highest embedded rocks, to cry thence.

Salut au Monde!
What cities the light or warmth penetrates, I penetrate
    those cities myself;
All islands to which birds wing their way, I wing my way
    myself.

Toward all
I raise high the perpendicular hand—I make the signal,
To remain after me in sight for ever,
For all the haunts and homes of men.

A BROADWAY PAGEANT.

(Reception of the Japanese Embassy, June 16, 1860.)

1.

Over sea, hither from Niphon,
Courteous, the Princes of Asia, swart-cheeked princes,
First-comers, guests, two-sworded princes,
Lesson-giving princes, leaning back in their open
    barouches, bare-headed, impassive,
This day they ride through Manhattan.

2.

Libertad!
I do not know whether others behold what I behold,
In the procession, along with the Princes of Asia, the
    errand-bearers,
Bringing up the rear, hovering above, around, or in the
    ranks marching;
But I will sing you a song of what I behold, Libertad.

3.

When million-footed Manhattan, unpent, descends to its
    pavements;
When the thunder-cracking guns arouse me with the
    proud roar I love;

When the round-mouthed guns, out of the smoke and
    smell I love, spit their salutes;
When the fire-flashing guns have fully alerted me—when
    heaven-clouds canopy my city with a delicate thin
    haze;
When, gorgeous, the countless straight stems, the forests
    at the wharves, thicken with colours;
When every ship, richly dressed, carries her flag at the
    peak;
When pennants trail, and street-festoons hang from the
    windows;
When Broadway is entirely given up to foot-passengers
    and foot-standers—
when the mass is densest;
When the façades of the houses are alive with people—
    when eyes gaze, riveted, tens of thousands at a time;
When the guests from the islands advance—when the
    pageant moves forward, visible;
When the summons is made—when the answer, that
    waited thousands of years, answers;
I too, arising, answering, descend to the pavements,
    merge with the crowd, and gaze with them.

4.

Superb-faced Manhattan!
Comrade Americanos!—to us, then, at last, the Orient
    comes.

To us, my city,
Where our tall-topped marble and iron beauties range on
    opposite sides—to walk in the space between,
To-day our Antipodes comes.

The Originatress comes,

The land of Paradise—land of the Caucasus—the nest of
    birth,
The nest of languages, the bequeather of poems, the race
    of eld,
Florid with blood, pensive, rapt with musings, hot with
    passion,
Sultry with perfume, with ample and flowing garments,
With sunburnt visage, with intense soul and glittering
    eyes,
The race of Brahma comes!

See, my cantabile! these, and more, are flashing to us from
    the procession;
As it moves changing, a kaleidoscope divine it moves
    changing before us.

Not the errand-bearing princes, nor the tanned Japanee
    only;
Lithe and silent, the Hindoo appears—the whole Asiatic
    continent itself appears—the Past, the dead,
The murky night-morning of wonder and fable,
    inscrutable,
The enveloped mysteries, the old and unknown hive-bees,
The North—the sweltering South—Assyria—the
    Hebrews—the Ancient of ancients,
Vast desolated cities—the gliding Present—all of these,
    and more, are in the pageant-procession.

Geography, the world, is in it;
The Great Sea, the brood of islands, Polynesia, the coast
    beyond;
The coast you henceforth are facing—you Libertad! from
    your Western golden shores;
The countries there, with their populations—the millions
    en masse, are curiously here;

The swarming market-places—the temples, with idols
    ranged along the sides, or at the end—bronze,
    brahmin, and lama;
The mandarin, farmer, merchant, mechanic, and
    fisherman;
The singing-girl and the dancing-girl—the ecstatic
    person—the divine Buddha;
The secluded Emperors—Confucius himself—the great
    poets and heroes—the warriors, the castes, all,
Trooping up, crowding from all directions—from the
    Altay mountains,
From Thibet—from the four winding and far-flowing
    rivers of China,
From the Southern peninsulas, and the demi-continental
    islands—from Malaysia;
These, and whatever belongs to them, palpable, show forth
    to me, and are seized by me,
And I am seized by them, and friendlily held by them,
Till, as here, them all I chant, Libertad! for themselves
    and for you.

5.

For I too, raising my voice, join the ranks of this pageant;
I am the chanter—I chant aloud over the pageant;
I chant the world on my Western Sea;
I chant, copious, the islands beyond, thick as stars in the
    sky;
I chant the new empire, grander than any before—As in a
    vision it comes to me;
I chant America, the Mistress—I chant a greater
    supremacy;
I chant, projected, a thousand blooming cities yet, in time,
    on those groups of sea-islands;

I chant my sail-ships and steam-ships threading the
    archipelagoes;
I chant my stars and stripes fluttering in the wind;
I chant commerce opening, the sleep of ages having done
    its work—races reborn, refreshed;
Lives, works, resumed—The object I know not—but the
    old, the Asiatic, resumed, as it must be,
Commencing from this day, surrounded by the world.

And you, Libertad of the world!
You shall sit in the middle, well-poised, thousands of
    years;
As to-day, from one side, the Princes of Asia come to you;
As to-morrow, from the other side, the Queen of England
    sends her eldest son to you.

The sign is reversing, the orb is enclosed,
The ring is circled, the journey is done;
The box-lid is but perceptibly opened—nevertheless the
    perfume pours copiously out of the whole box.

6.

Young Libertad!
With the venerable Asia, the all-mother,
Be considerate with her, now and ever, hot Libertad—for
    you are all;
Bend your proud neck to the long-off mother, now
    sending messages over the archipelagoes to you:
Bend your proud neck for once, young Libertad.

7.

Were the children straying westward so long? so wide the
    tramping?

Were the precedent dim ages debouching westward from
    Paradise so long?
Were the centuries steadily footing it that way, all the
    while unknown, for you, for reasons?
They are justified—they are accomplished—they shall
    now be turned the other way also, to travel toward
    you thence;
They shall now also march obediently eastward, for your
    sake, Libertad.

OLD IRELAND.

1.

Far hence, amid an isle of wondrous beauty,
Crouching over a grave, an ancient sorrowful mother,
Once a queen—now lean and tattered, seated on the
    ground,
Her old white hair drooping dishevelled round her
    shoulders;
At her feet fallen an unused royal harp,
Long silent—she too long silent—mourning her shrouded
    hope and heir;
Of all the earth her heart most full of sorrow, because
    most full of love.

2.

Yet a word, ancient mother;
You need crouch there no longer on the cold ground, with
    forehead between your knees;
O you need not sit there, veiled in your old white hair, so
    dishevelled;
For know you, the one you mourn is not in that grave;
It was an illusion—the heir, the son you love, was not
    really dead;
The Lord is not dead—he is risen again, young and strong,
    in another country;
Even while you wept there by your fallen harp, by the
    grave,
What you wept for was translated, passed from the grave,

The winds favoured, and the sea sailed it,
And now, with rosy and new blood,
Moves to-day in a new country.

BOSTON TOWN.

1.

To get betimes in Boston town, I rose this morning early;
Here's a good place at the corner—I must stand and see
the show.

2.

Clear the way there, Jonathan!
Way for the President's marshal! Way for the government
cannon!
Way for the Federal foot and dragoons—and the
apparitions copiously tumbling.

I love to look on the stars and stripes—I hope the fifes will
play "Yankee Doodle,"

How bright shine the cutlasses of the foremost troops!
Every man holds his revolver, marching stiff through
Boston town.

3.

A fog follows—antiques of the same come limping,
Some appear wooden-legged, and some appear bandaged
and bloodless.

Why this is indeed a show! It has called the dead out of
the earth!

The old graveyards of the hills have hurried to see!
Phantoms! phantoms countless by flank and rear!
Cocked hats of mothy mould! crutches made of mist!
Arms in slings! old men leaning on young men's
    shoulders!

What troubles you, Yankee phantoms? What is all this
    chattering of bare gums?
Does the ague convulse your limbs? Do you mistake your
    crutches for firelocks, and level them?

If you blind your eyes with tears, you will not see the
    President's marshal;
If you groan such groans, you might baulk the
    government cannon.

For shame, old maniacs! Bring down those tossed arms,
    and let your white hair be;
Here gape your great grandsons—their wives gaze at
    them from the windows,
See how well-dressed—see how orderly they conduct
    themselves.

Worse and worse! Can't you stand it? Are you retreating?
Is this hour with the living too dead for you?

Retreat then! Pell-mell!
To your graves! Back! back to the hills, old limpers!
I do not think you belong here, anyhow.

4.

But there is one thing that belongs here—shall I tell you
    what it is, gentlemen of Boston?

I will whisper it to the Mayor—He shall send a
    committee to England;
They shall get a grant from the Parliament, go with a cart
    to the royal vault—haste!
Dig out King George's coffin, unwrap him quick from the
    grave-clothes, box up his bones for a journey;

Find a swift Yankee clipper—here is freight for you,
    black-bellied clipper,
Up with your anchor! shake out your sails! steer straight
    toward Boston bay.

5.

Now call for the President's marshal again, bring out the
    government cannon,

Fetch home the roarers from Congress,—make another
    procession, guard it with foot and dragoons.

This centre-piece for them!
Look, all orderly citizens! Look from the windows,
    women!

The committee open the box; set up the regal ribs; glue
    those that will not stay;
Clap the skull on top of the ribs, and clap a crown on top
    of the skull.

You have got your revenge, old bluster! The crown is
    come to its own, and more than its own.

6.

Stick your hands in your pockets, Jonathan—you are a
    made man from this day;
You are mighty 'cute—and here is one of your bargains.

FRANCE,

The 18th year of these States.[1]

1.

A great year and place;
A harsh, discordant, natal scream out-sounding, to touch
the mother's heart closer than any yet.

2.

I walked the shores of my Eastern Sea,
Heard over the waves the little voice, S
aw the divine infant, where she woke, mournfully
wailing, amid the roar of cannon, curses, shouts,
crash of falling buildings;
Was not so sick from the blood in the gutters running—
nor from the single corpses, nor those in heaps, nor
those borne away in the tumbrils;
Was not so desperate at the battues of death—was not so
shocked at the repeated fusillades of the guns.

Pale, silent, stern, what could I say to that long-accrued
retribution?
Could I wish humanity different?
Could I wish the people made of wood and stone?
Or that there be no justice in destiny or time?

3.

O Liberty! O mate for me!
Here too the blaze, the bullet, and the axe, in reserve to
    fetch them out in case of need,
Here too, though long repressed, can never be destroyed;
Here too could rise at last, murdering and ecstatic;
Here too demanding full arrears of vengeance.

Hence I sign this salute over the sea,
And I do not deny that terrible red birth and baptism,
But remember the little voice that I heard wailing—and
    wait with perfect trust, no matter how long;
And from to-day, sad and cogent, I maintain the
    bequeathed cause, as for all lands,
And I send these words to Paris with my love,
And I guess some *chansonniers* there will understand
    them,
For I guess there is latent music yet in France—floods of
    it.
O I hear already the bustle of instruments—they will
    soon be drowning all that would interrupt them;
O I think the east wind brings a triumphal and free
    march,
It reaches hither—it swells me to joyful madness,
I will run transpose it in words, to justify it,
I will yet sing a song for you, *ma femme!*

FOOTNOTES:

1. *1793-4—-The great poet of Democracy is "not so shocked" at the
great European year of Democracy.*

EUROPE,

———————————

The 72nd and 73rd years of these States.[1]

1.

Suddenly, out of its stale and drowsy lair, the lair of slaves,
Like lightning it leaped forth, half startled at itself,
Its feet upon the ashes and the rags—its hands tight to the
 throats of kings.

O hope and faith!
O aching close of exiled patriots' lives!
O many a sickened heart!
Turn back unto this day, and make yourselves afresh.

2.

And you, paid to defile the People! you liars, mark!
Not for numberless agonies, murders, lusts,
For court thieving in its manifold mean forms, worming
 from his simplicity the poor man's wages,
For many a promise sworn by royal lips, and broken, and
 laughed at in the breaking,
Then in their power, not for all these did the blows strike
 revenge, or the heads of the nobles fall;
The People scorned the ferocity of kings.

3.

But the sweetness of mercy brewed bitter destruction, and
    the frightened rulers come back;
Each comes in state with his train—hangman, priest, tax-
    gatherer,
Soldier, lawyer, lord, jailer, and sycophant.

4.

Yet behind all, lowering, stealing—lo, a Shape,
Vague as the night, draped interminably, head, front, and
    form, in scarlet folds,
Whose face and eyes none may see:
Out of its robes only this—the red robes, lifted by the
    arm—
One finger crooked, pointed high over the top, like the
    head of a snake appears.

5.

Meanwhile, corpses lie in new-made graves—bloody
    corpses of young men;
The rope of the gibbet hangs heavily, the bullets of princes
    are flying, the creatures of power laugh aloud,
And all these things bear fruits—and they are good.

Those corpses of young men,
Those martyrs that hang from the gibbets—those hearts
    pierced by the grey lead,
Cold and motionless as they seem, live elsewhere with
    unslaughtered vitality.

They live in other young men, O kings!
They live in brothers, again ready to defy you!

They were purified by death—they were taught and
    exalted.

Not a grave of the murdered for freedom but grows seed
    for freedom, in its turn to bear seed,
Which the winds carry afar and resow, and the rains and
    the snows nourish.
Not a disembodied spirit can the weapons of tyrants let
    loose,
But it stalks invisibly over the earth, whispering,
    counselling, cautioning.

6.

Liberty! let others despair of you! I never despair of you.

Is the house shut? Is the master away?
Nevertheless, be ready—be not weary of watching:
He will soon return—his messengers come anon.

FOOTNOTES :

1. *The years 1848 and 1849.*

TO A
FOILED REVOLTER
OR REVOLTRESS.

1.

Courage! my brother or my sister!
Keep on! Liberty is to be subserved, whatever occurs;
That is nothing that is quelled by one or two failures, or
    any number of failures,
Or by the indifference or ingratitude of the people, or by
    any unfaithfulness,
Or the show of the tushes of power, soldiers, cannon,
    penal statutes.

2.

What we believe in waits latent for ever through all the
    continents, and all the islands and archipelagoes of
    the sea.

What we believe in invites no one, promises nothing,
    sits in calmness and light, is positive and composed,
    knows no discouragement,
Waiting patiently, waiting its time.

3.

The battle rages with many a loud alarm, and frequent
    advance and retreat,
The infidel triumphs—or supposes he triumphs,

The prison, scaffold, garrote, handcuffs, iron necklace and
    anklet, lead- balls, do their work,
The named and unnamed heroes pass to other spheres,
The great speakers and writers are exiled—they lie sick in
    distant lands,
The cause is asleep—the strongest throats are still, choked
with their own blood,
The young men drop their eyelashes toward the ground
    when they meet;
But, for all this, Liberty has not gone out of the place, nor
    the infidel entered into possession.

When Liberty goes out of a place, it is not the first to go,
    nor the second or third to go,
It waits for all the rest to go—it is the last.

When there are no more memories of heroes and martyrs,
And when all life and all the souls of men and women are
    discharged from any part of the earth,
Then only shall Liberty be discharged from that part of
    the earth,
And the infidel and the tyrant come into possession.

4.

Then courage! revolter! revoltress!
For till all ceases neither must you cease.

5.

I do not know what you are for, (I do not know what I am
    for myself, nor what anything is for,)
But I will search carefully for it even in being foiled,
In defeat, poverty, imprisonment—for they too are great.

Did we think victory great?
So it is—But now it seems to me, when it cannot be
    helped, that defeat is great,
And that death and dismay are great.

DRUM TAPS.

MANHATTAN ARMING.

1.

First, O songs, for a prelude,
Lightly strike on the stretched tympanum, pride and joy
  in my city,
How she led the rest to arms—how she gave the cue,
How at once with lithe limbs, unwaiting a moment, she
  sprang;
O superb! O Manhattan, my own, my peerless!
O strongest you in the hour of danger, in crisis! O truer
  than steel!
How you sprang! how you threw off the costumes of peace
  with indifferent hand;
How your soft opera-music changed, and the drum and
  fife were heard in their stead;
How you led to the war, (that shall serve for our prelude,
  songs of soldiers,)
How Manhattan drum-taps led.

2.

Forty years had I in my city seen soldiers parading;
Forty years as a pageant—till unawares, the Lady of this
  teeming and turbulent city,
Sleepless, amid her ships, her houses, her incalculable
  wealth,
With her million children around her—suddenly,
At dead of night, at news from the South,
Incensed, struck with clenched hand the pavement.

A shock electric—the night sustained it;
Till, with ominous hum, our hive at daybreak poured out
    its myriads.

From the houses then, and the workshops, and through
    all the doorways,
Leaped they tumultuous—and lo! Manhattan arming.

3.

To the drum-taps prompt,
The young men falling in and arming;
The mechanics arming, the trowel, the jack-plane, the
    black-smith's hammer, tossed aside with precipitation;
The lawyer leaving his office, and arming—the judge
    leaving the court;
The driver deserting his waggon in the street, jumping
    down, throwing the reins abruptly down on the
    horses' backs;
The salesman leaving the store—the boss, book-keeper,
    porter, all leaving;
Squads gathering everywhere by common consent, and
    arming;
The new recruits, even boys—the old men show them how
    to wear their accoutrements—they buckle the straps
    carefully;
Outdoors arming—indoors arming—the flash of the
    musket-barrels;
The white tents cluster in camps—the armed sentries
    around—the sunrise cannon, and again at sunset;
Armed regiments arrive every day, pass through the city,
    and embark from the wharves;
How good they look, as they tramp down to the river,
    sweaty, with their guns on their shoulders!

How I love them! how I could hug them, with their brown
    faces, and their clothes and knapsacks covered with
    dust!
The blood of the city up—armed! armed! the cry
    everywhere;
The flags flung out from the steeples of churches, and
    from all the public buildings and stores;
The tearful parting—the mother kisses her son—the son
    kisses his mother;
Loth is the mother to part—yet not a word does she speak
    to detain him;
The tumultuous escort—the ranks of policemen
    preceding, clearing the way;
The unpent enthusiasm—the wild cheers of the crowd for
    their favourites;
The artillery—the silent cannons, bright as gold, drawn
    along, rumble lightly over the stones;
Silent cannons—soon to cease your silence,
Soon, unlimbered, to begin the red business!
All the mutter of preparation—all the determined
    arming;
The hospital service—the lint, bandages, and medicines;
The women volunteering for nurses—the work begun for,
    in earnest—no mere parade now;
War! an armed race is advancing!—the welcome for
    battle—no turning away;
War! be it weeks, months, or years—an armed race is
    advancing to welcome it.

4.

Mannahatta a-march!—and it's O to sing it well!
It's O for a manly life in the camp!

159

5.

And the sturdy artillery!
The guns, bright as gold—the work for giants—to serve
    well the guns:
Unlimber them! no more, as the past forty years, for
    salutes for courtesies merely;
Put in something else now besides powder and wadding.

6.

And you, Lady of Ships! you, Mannahatta!
Old matron of the city! this proud, friendly, turbulent
    city!
Often in peace and wealth you were pensive, or covertly
    frowned amid all your children;
But now you smile with joy, exulting old Mannahatta!

1861.

Armed year! year of the struggle!
No dainty rhymes or sentimental love verses for you,
    terrible year!
Not you as some pale poetling, seated at a desk, lisping
    cadenzas piano;
But as a strong man, erect, clothed in blue clothes,
    advancing, carrying a rifle on your shoulder,
With well-gristled body and sunburnt face and hands—
    with a knife in the belt at your side,

As I heard you shouting loud—your sonorous voice
    ringing across the continent;
Your masculine voice, O year, as rising amid the great
    cities,
Amid the men of Manhattan I saw you, as one of the
    workmen, the dwellers in Manhattan;
Or with large steps crossing the prairies out of Illinois and
    Indiana,
Rapidly crossing the West with springy gait, and
    descending the Alleghanies;
Or down from the great lakes, or in Pennsylvania, or on
    deck along the Ohio river;
Or southward along the Tennessee or Cumberland rivers,
    or at Chattanooga on the mountain-top,
Saw I your gait and saw I your sinewy limbs, clothed in
    blue, bearing weapons, robust year;
Heard your determined voice, launched forth again and
    again;

Year that suddenly sang by the mouths of the round-
    lipped cannon,
I repeat you, hurrying, crashing, sad, distracted year.

THE UPRISING.

1.

Rise, O days, from your fathomless deeps, till you loftier
    and fiercer sweep!
Long for my soul, hungering gymnastic, I devoured what
    the earth gave me;
Long I roamed the woods of the North—long I watched
    Niagara pouring;
I travelled the prairies over, and slept on their breast—I
    crossed the Nevadas,
I crossed the plateaus;
I ascended the towering rocks along the Pacific, I sailed
    out to sea;
I sailed through the storm, I was refreshed by the storm;
I watched with joy the threatening maws of the waves;
I marked the white combs where they careered so high,
    curling over;
I heard the wind piping, I saw the black clouds;
Saw from below what arose and mounted, (O superb! O
    wild as my heart, and powerful!)
Heard the continuous thunder, as it bellowed after the
    lightning;
Noted the slender and jagged threads of lightning, as
    sudden and fast amid the din they chased each other
    across the sky;
—These, and such as these, I, elate, saw—saw with
    wonder, yet pensive and masterful;
All the menacing might of the globe uprisen around me;
Yet there with my soul I fed—I fed content, supercilious.

2.

'Twas well, O soul! 'twas a good preparation you gave me!
Now we advance our latent and ampler hunger to fill;
Now we go forth to receive what the earth and the sea
    never gave us;
Not through the mighty woods we go, but through the
    mightier cities;
Something for us is pouring now, more than Niagara
    pouring;
Torrents of men, (sources and rills of the North-west, are
    you indeed inexhaustible?)
What, to pavements and homesteads here—what were
    those storms of the mountains and sea?
What, to passions I witness around me to-day, was the sea
    risen?
Was the wind piping the pipe of death under the black
    clouds?
Lo! from deeps more unfathomable, something more
    deadly and savage;
Manhattan, rising, advancing with menacing front—
    Cincinnati, Chicago, unchained;
—What was that swell I saw on the ocean? behold what
    comes here!
How it climbs with daring feet and hands! how it dashes!
How the true thunder bellows after the lightning! how
    bright the flashes of lightning!
How DEMOCRACY with desperate vengeful port strides
    on, shown through the dark by those flashes of
    lightning!
Yet a mournful wail and low sob I fancied I heard through
    the dark,
In a lull of the deafening confusion.

3.

Thunder on! stride on, Democracy! strike with vengeful
    stroke!
And do you rise higher than ever yet, O days, O cities!
Crash heavier, heavier yet, O storms! you have done me
    good;
My soul, prepared in the mountains, absorbs your
    immortal strong nutriment.
Long had I walked my cities, my country roads, through
    farms, only half satisfied;
One doubt, nauseous, undulating like a snake, crawled on
    the ground before me,
Continually preceding my steps, turning upon me oft,
    ironically hissing low;
—The cities I loved so well I abandoned and left—I sped
    to the certainties suitable to me
Hungering, hungering, hungering, for primal energies,
    and Nature's dauntlessness,
I refreshed myself with it only, I could relish it only;
I waited the bursting forth of the pent fire—on the water
    and air I waited long.
—But now I no longer wait—I am fully satisfied—I am
    glutted;
I have witnessed the true lightning—I have witnessed my
    cities electric;
I have lived to behold man burst forth, and warlike
    America rise;
Hence I will seek no more the food of the northern
    solitary wilds,
No more on the mountains roam, or sail the stormy sea.

BEAT! BEAT! DRUMS!

1.

Beat! beat! drums!—Blow! bugles! blow!
Through the windows—through doors—burst like a force
  of ruthless men,
Into the solemn church, and scatter the congregation;
Into the school where the scholar is studying:
Leave not the bridegroom quiet—no happiness must he
  have now with his bride;
Nor the peaceful farmer any peace, ploughing his field or
  gathering his grain;
So fierce you whirr and pound, you drums—so shrill you
  bugles blow.

2.

Beat! beat! drums!—Blow! bugles! blow!
Over the traffic of cities—over the rumble of wheels in the
  streets:
Are beds prepared, for sleepers at night in the houses? No
  sleepers must sleep in those beds;
No bargainers' bargains by day—no brokers or
  speculators—Would they continue?
Would the talkers be talking? would the singer attempt to
  sing?
Would the lawyer rise in the court to state his case before
  the judge?
Then rattle quicker, heavier, drums—you bugles wilder
  blow.

3.

Beat! beat! drums!—Blow! bugles! blow!
Make no parley—stop for no expostulation;
Mind not the timid—mind not the weeper or prayer;
Mind not the old man beseeching the young man;
Let not the child's voice be heard, nor the mother's
    entreaties;
Make even the trestles to shake the dead, where they lie
    awaiting the hearses,
So strong you thump, O terrible drums—so loud you
    bugles blow.

SONG OF THE
BANNER AT DAYBREAK.

Poet.

O a new song, a free song,
Flapping, flapping, flapping, flapping, by sounds, by
  voices clearer,
By the wind's voice and that of the drum,
By the banner's voice, and child's voice, and sea's voice,
  and father's voice,
Low on the ground and high in the air,
On the ground where father and child stand,
In the upward air where their eyes turn,
Where the banner at daybreak is flapping.

Words! book-words! what are you?
Words no more, for hearken and see,
My song is there in the open air—and I must sing,
With the banner and pennant a-flapping.

I'll weave the chord and twine in,
Man's desire and babe's desire—I'll twine them in, I'll put
  in life;
I'll put the bayonet's flashing point—I'll let bullets and
  slugs whizz;
I'll pour the verse with streams of blood, full of volition,
  full of joy;
Then loosen, launch forth, to go and compete,
With the banner and pennant a-flapping.

Banner And Pennant.

Come up here, bard, bard;
Come up here, soul, soul;
Come up here, dear little child,
To fly in the clouds and winds with us, and play with the
  measureless light.

Child.

Father, what is that in the sky beckoning to me with long
  finger?
And what does it say to me all the while?

Father.

Nothing, my babe, you see in the sky;
And nothing at all to you it says. But look you, my babe,
Look at these dazzling things in the houses, and see you
  the money-shops opening;
And see you the vehicles preparing to crawl along the
  streets with goods:
These! ah, these! how valued and toiled for, these!
How envied by all the earth!

Poet.

Fresh and rosy red, the sun is mounting high;
On floats the sea in distant blue, careering through its
  channels;
On floats the wind over the breast of the sea, setting in
  toward land;
The great steady wind from west and west-by-south,
Floating so buoyant, with milk-white foam on the waters.

169

But I am not the sea, nor the red sun;
I am not the wind, with girlish laughter;
Not the immense wind which strengthens—not the wind
    which lashes;
Not the spirit that ever lashes its own body to terror and
    death:
But I am of that which unseen comes and sings, sings,
    sings,
Which babbles in brooks and scoots in showers on the
    land;
Which the birds know in the woods, mornings and
    evenings,
And the shore-sands know, and the hissing wave, and that
    banner and pennant,
Aloft there flapping and flapping.

Child.

O father, it is alive—it is full of people—it has children!
O now it seems to me it is talking to its children!
I hear it—it talks to me—O it is wonderful!
O it stretches—it spreads and runs so fast! O my father,
It is so broad it covers the whole sky!

Father.

Cease, cease, my foolish babe,
What you are saying is sorrowful to me—much it
    displeases me;
Behold with the rest, again I say—behold not banners and
    pennants aloft;
But the well-prepared pavements behold—and mark the
    solid-walled houses.

Banner And Pennant.

Speak to the child, O bard, out of Manhattan;
Speak to our children all, or north or south of Manhattan,
Where our factory-engines hum, where our miners delve
    the ground,
Where our hoarse Niagara rumbles, where our prairie-
    ploughs are ploughing;
Speak, O bard! point this day, leaving all the rest, to us
    over all—and yet we know not why;
For what are we, mere strips of cloth, profiting nothing,
Only flapping in the wind?

Poet.

I hear and see not strips of cloth alone;
I hear the tramp of armies, I hear the challenging sentry;
I hear the jubilant shouts of millions of men—I hear
    LIBERTY!
I hear the drums beat, and the trumpets blowing;
I myself move abroad, swift-rising, flying then;
I use the wings of the land-bird, and use the wings of the
    sea-bird, and look down as from a height.
I do not deny the precious results of peace—I see
    populous cities, with wealth incalculable;
I see numberless farms—I see the farmers working in
    their fields or barns;
I see mechanics working—I see buildings everywhere
    founded, going up, or finished;
I see trains of cars swiftly speeding along railroad tracks,
    drawn by the locomotives;
I see the stores, depots, of Boston, Baltimore, Charleston,
    New Orleans;
I see far in the west the immense area of grain—I dwell a
    while, hovering;

I pass to the lumber forests of the north, and again to the
    southern plantation, and again to California;
Sweeping the whole, I see the countless profit, the busy
    gatherings, earned wages;
See the identity formed out of thirty-six spacious and
    haughty States, (and many more to come;)
See forts on the shores of harbours—see ships sailing in
    and out;
Then over all, (aye! aye!) my little and lengthened pennant
    shaped like a sword
Runs swiftly up, indicating war and defiance—And now
    the halyards have raised it,
Side of my banner broad and blue—side of my starry
    banner,
Discarding peace over all the sea and land.

Banner And Pennant.

Yet louder, higher, stronger, bard! yet farther, wider
    cleave!
No longer let our children deem us riches and peace
    alone;
We can be terror and carnage also, and are so now.
Not now are we one of these spacious and haughty States,
    (nor any five, nor ten;)
Nor market nor depot are we, nor money-bank in the city;
But these, and all, and the brown and spreading land, and
    the mines below, are ours;
And the shores of the sea are ours, and the rivers great
    and small;
And the fields they moisten are ours, and the crops, and
    the fruits are ours;
Bays and channels, and ships sailing in and out, are
    ours—and we over all,

Over the area spread below, the three millions of square
    miles—the capitals,
The thirty-five millions of people—O bard! in life and
    death supreme,
We, even we, from this day flaunt out masterful, high up
    above,
Not for the present alone, for a thousand years, chanting
    through you
This song to the soul of one poor little child.

Child.

O my father, I like not the houses;
They will never to me be anything—nor do I like money!
But to mount up there I would like, O father dear—that
    banner I like;
That pennant I would be, and must be.

Father.

Child of mine, you fill me with anguish,
To be that pennant would be too fearful;
Little you know what it is this day, and henceforth for
    ever;
It is to gain nothing, but risk and defy everything;
Forward to stand in front of wars—and O, such wars!—
    what have you to do with them?
With passions of demons, slaughter, premature death?

Poet.

Demons and death then I sing;
Put in all, aye all, will I—sword-shaped pennant for war,
    and banner so broad and blue,

173

And a pleasure new and ecstatic, and the prattled
  yearning of children,
Blent with the sounds of the peaceful land, and the liquid
  wash of the sea;
And the icy cool of the far, far north, with rustling cedars
  and pines;
And the whirr of drums, and the sound of soldiers
  marching, and the hot sun shining south;
And the beach-waves combing over the beach on my
  eastern shore, and my western shore the same;
And all between those shores, and my ever-running
  Mississippi, with bends and chutes;
And my Illinois fields, and my Kansas fields, and my
  fields of Missouri;
The CONTINENT—devoting the whole identity, without
  reserving an atom,
Pour in! whelm that which asks, which sings, with all, and
  the yield of all.

Banner And Pennant.

Aye all! for ever, for all!
From sea to sea, north and south, east and west,
Fusing and holding, claiming, devouring the whole;
No more with tender lip, nor musical labial sound,
But out of the night emerging for good, our voice
  persuasive no more,
Croaking like crows here in the wind.

Poet.

My limbs, my veins dilate;
The blood of the world has filled me full—my theme is
  clear at last.

—Banner so broad, advancing out of the night, I sing you
    haughty and resolute;
I burst through where I waited long, too long, deafened
    and blinded;
My sight, my hearing and tongue, are come to me, (a little
    child taught me;)
I hear from above, O pennant of war, your ironical call
    and demand;
Insensate! insensate! yet I at any rate chant you, O banner!
Not houses of peace are you, nor any nor all their
    prosperity; if need be, you shall have every one of
    those houses to destroy them;
You thought not to destroy those valuable houses,
    standing fast, full of comfort, built with money;
May they stand fast, then? Not an hour, unless you, above
    them and all, stand fast.
—O banner! not money so precious are you, nor farm
    produce you, nor the material good nutriment,
Nor excellent stores, nor landed on wharves from the
    ships;
Not the superb ships, with sail-power or steam-power,
    fetching and carrying cargoes,
Nor machinery, vehicles, trade, nor revenues,—But you,
    as henceforth I see you,
Running up out of the night, bringing your cluster of
    stars, ever-enlarging stars;
Divider of daybreak you, cutting the air, touched by the
    sun, measuring the sky,
Passionately seen and yearned for by one poor little child,
While others remain busy, or smartly talking, for ever
    teaching thrift, thrift;
O you up there! O pennant! where you undulate like a
    snake, hissing so curious,
Out of reach—an idea only—yet furiously fought for,
    risking bloody death—loved by me!

So loved! O you banner, leading the day, with stars
  brought from the night!
Valueless, object of eyes, over all and demanding all—O
  banner and pennant!
I too leave the rest—great as it is, it is nothing—houses,
  machines are nothing—I see them not;
I see but you, O warlike pennant! O banner so broad, with
  stripes, I sing you only,
Flapping up there in the wind.

THE BIVOUAC'S FLAME.

By the bivouac's fitful flame,
A procession winding around me, solemn and sweet and
    slow;—but first I note
The tents of the sleeping army, the fields' and woods' dim
    outline,
The darkness, lit by spots of kindled fire—the silence;
Like a phantom far or near an occasional figure moving;
The shrubs and trees, (as I lift my eyes they seem to be
    stealthily watching me;)
While wind in procession thoughts, O tender and
    wondrous thoughts,
Of life and death—of home and the past and loved, and of
    those that are far away;
A solemn and slow procession there as I sit on the ground,
By the bivouac's fitful flame.

BIVOUAC ON
A MOUNTAIN-SIDE.

———————

I see before me now a travelling army halting;
Below, a fertile valley spread, with barns, and the orchards
    of summer;
Behind, the terraced sides of a mountain, abrupt in places,
    rising high;
Broken with rocks, with clinging cedars, with tall shapes,
    dingily seen;
The numerous camp-fires scattered near and far, some
    away up on the mountain;
The shadowy forms of men and horses, looming, large-
    sized, flickering;
And over all, the sky—the sky! far, far out of reach,
    studded with the eternal stars.

CITY OF SHIPS.

City of ships!
(O the black ships! O the fierce ships!
O the beautiful, sharp-bowed steam-ships and sail-ships!)
City of the world! (for all races are here;
All the lands of the earth make contributions here;)
City of the sea! city of hurried and glittering tides!
City whose gleeful tides continually rush or recede,
    whirling in and out, with eddies and foam!
City of wharves and stores! city of tall façades of marble
    and iron!
Proud and passionate city! mettlesome, mad, extravagant
    city!
Spring up, O city! not for peace alone, but be indeed
    yourself, warlike!
Fear not! submit to no models but your own, O city!
Behold me! incarnate me, as I have incarnated you!
I have rejected nothing you offered me—whom you
    adopted, I have adopted;
Good or bad, I never question you—I love all—I do not
    condemn anything;
I chant and celebrate all that is yours—yet peace no more;
In peace I chanted peace, but now the drum of war is
    mine;
War, red war, is my song through your streets, O city!

VIGIL ON THE FIELD.

VIGIL strange I kept on the field one night,
When you, my son and my comrade, dropped at my side
    that day.
One look I but gave, which your dear eyes returned with a
    look I shall never forget;
One touch of your hand to mine, O boy, reached up as
    you lay on the ground.
Then onward I sped in the battle, the even-contested
    battle;
Till, late in the night relieved, to the place at last again I
    made my way;
Found you in death so cold, dear comrade—found your
    body, son of responding kisses, (never again on earth
    responding;)
Bared your face in the starlight—curious the scene—cool
    blew the moderate night-wind.
Long there and then in vigil I stood, dimly around me the
    battlefield spreading;
Vigil wondrous and vigil sweet, there in the fragrant
    silent night.
But not a tear fell, not even a long-drawn sigh—Long,
    long I gazed;
Then on the earth partially reclining, sat by your side,
    leaning my chin in my hands;
Passing sweet hours, immortal and mystic hours, with
    you, dearest comrade—
Not a tear, not a word;
Vigil of silence, love, and death—vigil for you, my son and
    my soldier,

As onward silently stars aloft, eastward new ones upward
    stole;
Vigil final for you, brave boy, (I could not save you, swift
    was your death,
I faithfully loved you and cared for you living—I think we
    shall surely meet again;)
Till at latest lingering of the night, indeed just as the dawn
    appeared,
My comrade I wrapped in his blanket, enveloped well his
    form,
Folded the blanket well, tucking it carefully over head,
    and carefully under feet;
And there and then, and bathed by the rising sun, my son
    in his grave, in his rude-dug grave, I deposited;
Ending my vigil strange with that—vigil of night and
    battlefield dim;
Vigil for boy of responding kisses, never again on earth
    responding;
Vigil for comrade swiftly slain, vigil I never forget—how
    as day brightened
I rose from the chill ground, and folded my soldier well in
    his blanket,
And buried him where he fell.

THE FLAG.

Bathed in war's perfume—delicate flag!
O to hear you call the sailors and the soldiers! flag like a
    beautiful woman!
O to hear the tramp, tramp, of a million answering men!
    O the ships they arm with joy!
O to see you leap and beckon from the tall masts of ships!
O to see you peering down on the sailors on the decks!
Flag like the eyes of women.

THE WOUNDED.

A march in the ranks hard-pressed, and the road
    unknown;
A route through a heavy wood, with muffled steps in the
    darkness;
Our army foiled with loss severe, and the sullen remnant
    retreating;
Till after midnight glimmer upon us the lights of a dim-
    lighted building;
We come to an open space in the woods, and halt by the
    dim-lighted building.
'Tis a large old church, at the crossing roads—'tis now an
    impromptu hospital;
—Entering but for a minute, I see a sight beyond all the
    pictures and poems ever made:
Shadows of deepest, deepest black, just lit by moving,
    candles and lamps,
And by one great pitchy torch, stationary, with wild red
    flame, and clouds of smoke;
By these, crowds, groups of forms, vaguely I see, on the
    floor, some in the pews laid down;
At my feet more distinctly, a soldier, a mere lad, in danger
    of bleeding to death, (he is shot in the abdomen;)
I staunch the blood temporarily, (the youngster's face is
    white as a lily;)
Then before I depart I sweep my eyes o'er the scene, fain
    to absorb it all;
Faces, varieties, postures, beyond description, most in
    obscurity, some of them dead;

Surgeons operating, attendants holding lights, the smell
   of ether, the odour of blood;
The crowd, O the crowd of the bloody forms of soldiers—
   the yard outside also filled;
Some on the bare ground, some on planks or stretchers,
   some in the death- spasm sweating;
An occasional scream or cry, the doctor's shouted orders
   or calls;
The glisten of the little steel instruments catching the
   glint of the torches;
These I resume as I chant—I see again the forms, I smell
   the odour;
Then hear outside the orders given, *Fall in, my men, Fall
   in.*
But first I bend to the dying lad—his eyes open—a half-
   smile gives he me;
Then the eyes close, calmly close: and I speed forth to the
   darkness,
Resuming, marching, as ever in darkness marching, on
   in the ranks,
The unknown road still marching.

A SIGHT IN CAMP.

1.

A sight in camp in the daybreak grey and dim,
As from my tent I emerge so early, sleepless,
As slow I walk in the cool fresh air the path near by the
    hospital tent,
Three forms I see on stretchers lying, brought out there,
    untended lying;
Over each the blanket spread, ample brownish woollen
    blanket,
Grey and heavy blanket, folding, covering all.

2.

Curious, I halt, and silent stand;
Then with light fingers I from the face of the nearest, the
    first, just lift the blanket;

Who are you, elderly man, so gaunt and grim, with well-
    greyed hair, and flesh all sunken about the eyes?
Who are you, my dear comrade?

Then to the second I step—And who are you, my child
    and darling?
Who are you, sweet boy, with cheeks yet blooming?

Then to the third—a face nor child nor old, very calm, as
    of beautiful yellow-white ivory:

Young man, I think I know you—I think this face of
    yours is the face of the Christ Himself;
Dead and divine and brother of all, and here again He
    lies.

A GRAVE.

1.

As toilsome I wandered Virginia's woods,
To the music of rustling leaves kicked by my feet—for
    'twas autumn—
I marked at the foot of a tree the grave of a soldier;
Mortally wounded he, and buried on the retreat—easily
    all could I understand;
The halt of a mid-day hour—when, Up! no time to lose!
    Yet this sign left
On a tablet scrawled and nailed on the tree by the grave,
Bold, cautious, true, and my loving comrade.

2.

Long, long I muse,—then on my way go wandering,
Many a changeful season to follow, and many a scene of
    life.
Yet at times through changeful season and scene,
    abrupt,—alone, or in the crowded street,—
Comes before me the unknown soldier's grave, comes the
    inscription rude in Virginia's woods,
Bold, cautious, true, and my loving comrade.

THE DRESSER.

1.

An old man bending, I come among new faces,
Years, looking backward, resuming, in answer to
    children,
"Come tell us, old man," (as from young men and maidens
    that love me,)
Years hence "of these scenes, of these furious passions,
    these chances,
Of unsurpassed heroes—(was one side so brave? the other
    was equally brave)
Now be witness again—paint the mightiest armies of
    earth;
Of those armies, so rapid, so wondrous, what saw you to
    tell us?
What stays with you latest and deepest? of curious panics,
Of hard-fought engagements, or sieges tremendous, what
    deepest remains?"

2.

O maidens and young men I love, and that love me,
What you ask of my days, those the strangest and sudden
    your talking recalls,
Soldier alert I arrive, after a long march, covered with
    sweat and dust;
In the nick of time I come, plunge in the fight, loudly
    shout in the rush of successful charge;

Enter the captured works,...yet lo! like a swift-running
    river, they fade,
Pass, and are gone; they fade—I dwell not on soldiers'
    perils or soldiers' joys;
(Both I remember well—many the hardships, few the joys,
    yet I was content.)

But in silence, in dreams' projections,
While the world of gain and appearance and mirth goes
    on,
So soon what is over forgotten, and waves wash the
    imprints off the sand,
In nature's reverie sad, with hinged knees returning, I
    enter the doors—(while for you up there, Whoever
    you are, follow me without noise, and be of strong
    heart.)
Bearing the bandages, water, and sponge,
Straight and swift to my wounded I go,
Where they lie on the ground, after the battle brought in;
Where their priceless blood reddens the grass, the
    ground;
Or to the rows of the hospital tent, or under the roofed
    hospital;
To the long rows of cots, up and down, each side, I return;
To each and all, one after another, I draw near—not one
    do I miss;
An attendant follows, holding a tray—he carries a refuse-
    pail,
Soon to be filled with clotted rags and blood, emptied,
    and filled again.

I onward go, I stop,
With hinged knees and steady hand, to dress wounds;
I am firm with each—the pangs are sharp, yet
    unavoidable;

One turns to me his appealing eyes—poor boy! I never
    knew you,
Yet I think I could not refuse this moment to die for you if
    that would save you.
On, on I go—(open, doors of time! open, hospital doors!)
The crushed head I dress (poor crazed hand, tear not the
    bandage away;)
The neck of the cavalry-man, with the bullet through and
    through, I examine;
Hard the breathing rattles, quite glazed already the eye,
    yet life struggles hard;
Come, sweet death! be persuaded, O beautiful death!
In mercy come quickly.

From the stump of the arm, the amputated hand,
I undo the clotted lint, remove the slough, wash off the
    matter and blood;
Back on his pillow the soldier bends, with curved neck,
    and side-falling head;
His eyes are closed, his face is pale, he dares not look on
    the bloody stump,
And has not yet looked on it.

I dress a wound in the side, deep, deep;
But a day or two more—for see, the frame all wasted and
    sinking,
And the yellow-blue countenance see.

I dress the perforated shoulder, the foot with the bullet
    wound,
Cleanse the one with a gnawing and putrid gangrene, so
    sickening, so offensive,
While the attendant stands behind aside me, holding the
    tray and pail.

I am faithful, I do not give out;
The fractured thigh, the knee, the wound in the abdomen,
These and more I dress with impassive hand—yet deep in
    my breast a fire, a burning flame.

3.

Thus in silence, in dreams' projections,
Returning, resuming, I thread my way through the
    hospitals;
The hurt and the wounded I pacify with soothing hand,
I sit by the restless all the dark night—some are so young,
Some suffer so much—I recall the experience sweet and
    sad.
Many a soldier's loving arms about this neck have crossed
    and rested,
Many a soldier's kiss dwells on these bearded lips.

A LETTER FROM CAMP.

1.

"Come up from the fields, father, here's a letter from our
    Pete;
And come to the front door, mother—here's a letter from
    thy dear son."

2.

Lo, 'tis autumn;
Lo, where the trees, deeper green, yellower and redder,
Cool and sweeten Ohio's villages, with leaves fluttering in
    the moderate wind;
Where apples ripe in the orchards hang, and grapes on
    the trellised vines;
Smell you the smell of the grapes on the vines?
Smell you the buckwheat, where the bees were lately
    buzzing?

Above all, lo, the sky, so calm, so transparent after the
    rain, and with wondrous clouds; Below, too, all calm,
    all vital and beautiful—and the farm prospers well.

3.

Down in the fields all prospers well;
But now from the fields come, father—come at the
    daughter's call;

And come to the entry, mother—to the front door come,
    right away.

Fast as she can she hurries—something ominous—her
    steps trembling;
She does not tarry to smooth her white hair, nor adjust
    her cap.

4.

Open the envelope quickly;
O this is not our son's writing, yet his name is signed;
O a strange hand writes for our dear son—O stricken
    mother's soul!
All swims before her eyes—flashes with black—she
    catches the main words only;
Sentences broken—"*gun-shot wound in the breast, cavalry
    skirmish, taken to hospital,
At present low, but will soon be better.*"

5.

Ah, now the single figure to me,
Amid all teeming and wealthy Ohio, with all its cities and
    farms,
Sickly white in the face and dull in the head, very faint,
By the jamb of a door leans.

6.

"Grieve not so, dear mother," the just-grown daughter
    speaks through her sobs;
The little sisters huddle around, speechless and dismayed;
"See, dearest mother, the letter says Pete will soon be
    better."

7.

Alas! poor boy, he will never be better, (nor maybe needs
    to be better, that brave and simple soul;)
While they stand at home at the door, he is dead already;
The only son is dead.

But the mother needs to be better;
She, with thin form, presently dressed in black;
By day her meals untouched—then at night fitfully
    sleeping, often waking,
In the midnight waking, weeping, longing with one deep
    longing,
O that she might withdraw unnoticed—silent from life
    escape and withdraw,
To follow, to seek, to be with her dear dead son!

WAR DREAMS.

1.

In clouds descending, in midnight sleep, of many a face in
    battle,
Of the look at first of the mortally wounded, of that
    indescribable look,
Of the dead on their backs, with arms extended wide—
    I dream, I dream, I dream.

2.

Of scenes of nature, the fields and the mountains,
Of the skies so beauteous after the storm, and at night the
    moon so unearthly bright,
Shining sweetly, shining down, where we dig the trenches,
    and gather the heaps—
    I dream, I dream, I dream.

3.

Long have they passed, long lapsed—faces, and trenches,
    and fields:
Long through the carnage I moved with a callous
    composure, or away from the fallen
Onward I sped at the time. But now of their faces and
    forms, at night,
    I dream, I dream, I dream.

THE VETERAN'S VISION.

While my wife at my side lies slumbering, and the wars
    are over long,
And my head on the pillow rests at home, and the mystic
    midnight passes,
And through the stillness, through the dark, I hear, just
    hear, the breath of my infant,
There in the room, as I wake from sleep, this vision
    presses upon me.
The engagement opens there and then, in my busy brain
    unreal;
The skirmishers begin—they crawl cautiously ahead—I
    hear the irregular snap! snap!
I hear the sound of the different missiles—the short *t-h-t!*
    t-h-t! of the rifle-balls;
I see the shells exploding, leaving small white clouds—I
    hear the great shells shrieking as they pass;
The grape, like the hum and whirr of wind through the
    trees, (quick, tumultuous, now the contest rages!)
All the scenes at the batteries themselves rise in detail
    before me again;
The crashing and smoking—the pride of the men in their
    pieces;
The chief gunner ranges and sights his piece, and selects a
    fuse of the right time;
After firing, I see him lean aside, and look eagerly off to
    note the effect;
—Elsewhere I hear the cry of a regiment charging—
    the young colonel leads himself this time, with
    brandished sword;

I see the gaps cut by the enemy's volleys, quickly filled
    up—no delay;
I breathe the suffocating smoke—then the flat clouds
    hover low, concealing all;
Now a strange lull comes for a few seconds, not a shot
    fired on either side;
Then resumed, the chaos louder than ever, with eager
    calls, and orders of officers;
While from some distant part of the field the wind wafts
    to my ears a shout of applause, (some special success;)
And ever the sound of the cannon, far or near, rousing,
    even in dreams, a devilish exultation, and all the old
    mad joy, in the depths of my soul;
And ever the hastening of infantry shifting positions—
    batteries, cavalry, moving hither and thither;
The falling, dying, I heed not—the wounded, dripping
    and red, I heed not— some to the rear are hobbling;
Grime, heat, rush—aides-de-camp galloping by, or on a
    full run:
With the patter of small arms, the warning *s-s-t* of the
    rifles, (these in my vision I hear or see,)
And bombs bursting in air, and at night the vari-coloured
    rockets.

O TAN-FACED PRAIRIE BOY.

O tan-faced prairie boy!
Before you came to camp came many a welcome gift;
Praises and presents came, and nourishing food—till at
    last, among the recruits,
You came, taciturn, with nothing to give—we but looked
    on each other,
When lo! more than all the gifts of the world you gave me.

MANHATTAN FACES.

1.

Give me the splendid silent sun, with all his beams full-
    dazzling;
Give me juicy autumnal fruit, ripe and red from the
    orchard;
Give me a field where the unmowed grass grows;
Give me an arbour, give me the trellised grape;
Give me fresh corn and wheat—give me serene-moving
    animals, teaching content;
Give me nights perfectly quiet, as on high plateaus west of
    the Mississippi, and I looking up at the stars;
Give me odorous at sunrise a garden of beautiful flowers,
    where I can walk undisturbed;
Give me for marriage a sweet-breathed woman, of whom I
    should never tire;
Give me a perfect child—give me, away, aside from the
    noise of the world, a rural domestic life;
Give me to warble spontaneous songs, relieved, recluse by
    myself, for my own ears only;
Give me solitude—give me Nature—give me again,
    O Nature, your primal sanities!
—These, demanding to have them, tired with ceaseless
    excitement, and racked by the war-strife,
These to procure incessantly asking, rising in cries from
    my heart,
While yet incessantly asking, still I adhere to my city;
Day upon day, and year upon year, O city, walking your
    streets,

Where you hold me enchained a certain time, refusing to
    give me up,
Yet giving to make me glutted, enriched of soul—you give
    me for ever faces;
O I see what I sought to escape, confronting, reversing my
    cries;
I see my own soul trampling down what it asked for.

2.

Keep your splendid silent sun;
Keep your woods, O Nature, and the quiet places by the
    woods;
Keep your fields of clover and timothy, and your
    cornfields and orchards;
Keep the blossoming buckwheat fields, where the ninth-
    month bees hum.
Give me faces and streets! give me these phantoms
    incessant and endless along the *trottoirs*!
Give me interminable eyes! give me women! give me
    comrades and lovers by the thousand!
Let me see new ones every day! let me hold new ones by
    the hand every day!
Give me such shows! give me the streets of Manhattan!
Give me Broadway, with the soldiers marching—give me
    the sound of the trumpets and drums!
The soldiers in companies or regiments—some starting
    away, flushed and reckless;
Some, their time up, returning, with thinned ranks—
    young, yet very old, worn, marching, noticing
    nothing;
—Give me the shores and the wharves heavy-fringed with
    the black ships!
O such for me! O an intense life! O full to repletion, and
    varied!

The life of the theatre, bar-room, huge hotel, for me!
The saloon of the steamer, the crowded excursion, for me!
    the torchlight procession!
The dense brigade, bound for the war, with high-piled
    military waggons following;
People, endless, streaming, with strong voices, passions,
    pageants;
Manhattan streets, with their powerful throbs, with the
    beating drums, as now;
The endless and noisy chorus, the rustle and clank of
    muskets, even the sight of the wounded;
Manhattan crowds, with their turbulent musical chorus—
    with varied chorus and light of the sparkling eyes;
Manhattan faces and eyes for ever for me!

OVER THE CARNAGE.

1.

Over the carnage rose prophetic a voice,—
Be not disheartened—Affection shall solve the problems
    of Freedom yet;
Those who love each other shall become invincible—they
    shall yet make Columbia victorious.

Sons of the Mother of all! you shall yet be victorious!
You shall yet laugh to scorn the attacks of all the
    remainder of the earth.

No danger shall baulk Columbia's lovers;
If need be, a thousand shall sternly immolate themselves
    for one.

One from Massachusetts shall be a Missourian's comrade;
From Maine and from hot Carolina, and another an
    Oregonese, shall be friends triune,
More precious to each other than all the riches of the
    earth.

To Michigan, Florida perfumes shall tenderly come;
Not the perfumes of flowers, but sweeter, and wafted
    beyond death.

It shall be customary in the houses and streets to see
    manly affection;

The most dauntless and rude shall touch face to face
    lightly;
The dependence of Liberty shall be lovers,
The continuance of Equality shall be comrades.

These shall tie you and band you stronger than hoops of
    iron;
I, ecstatic, O partners! O lands! with the love of lovers tie
    you.

2.

Were you looking to be held together by the lawyers?
Or by an agreement on a paper? or by arms?
—Nay—nor the world nor any living thing will so cohere.

THE MOTHER OF ALL.

Pensive, on her dead gazing, I heard the Mother of all,
Desperate, on the torn bodies, on the forms covering the
     battlefields, gazing;

As she called to her earth with mournful voice while she
     stalked.
"Absorb them well, O my earth!" she cried—"I charge you,
     lose not my sons! lose not an atom;
And you, streams, absorb them well, taking their dear
     blood;
And you local spots, and you airs that swim above lightly,
And all you essences of soil and growth—and you, O my
     rivers' depths;
And you mountain-sides—and the woods where my dear
     children's blood, trickling, reddened;
And you trees, down in your roots, to bequeath to all
     future trees,
My dead absorb—my young men's beautiful bodies
     absorb—and their precious, precious, precious blood;
Which, holding in trust for me, faithfully back again give
     me, many a year hence,

In unseen essence and odour of surface and grass,
     centuries hence;
In blowing airs from the fields, back again give me my
     darlings—give my immortal heroes;
Exhale me them centuries hence—breathe me their
     breath—let not an atom be lost.

O years and graves! O air and soil! O my dead, an aroma
    sweet!
Exhale them, perennial, sweet death, years, centuries
    hence."

CAMPS OF GREEN.

1.

Not alone our camps of white, O soldiers,
When, as ordered forward, after a long march,
Footsore and weary, soon as the light lessens, we halt for
　　the night;
Some of us so fatigued, carrying the gun and knapsack,
　　dropping asleep in our tracks;
Others pitching the little tents, and the fires lit up begin
　　to sparkle;
Outposts of pickets posted, surrounding, alert through
　　the dark,
And a word provided for countersign, careful for safety;
Till to the call of the drummers at daybreak loudly
　　beating the drums,
We rise up refreshed, the night and sleep passed over, and
　　resume our journey,
Or proceed to battle.

2.

Lo! the camps of the tents of green,
Which the days of peace keep filling, and the days of war
　　keep filling,
With a mystic army, (is it too ordered forward? is it too
　　only halting a while,
Till night and sleep pass over?)

Now in those camps of green—in their tents dotting the
    world;
In the parents, children, husbands, wives, in them—in the
    old and young,
Sleeping under the sunlight, sleeping under the
    moonlight, content and silent there at last;
Behold the mighty bivouac-field and waiting-camp of us
    and ours and all,
Of our corps and generals all, and the President over the
    corps and generals all,
And of each of us, O soldiers, and of each and all in the
    ranks we fight,
There without hatred we shall all meet.

For presently, O soldiers, we too camp in our place in the
    bivouac-camps of green;
But we need not provide for outposts, nor word for the
    countersign,
Nor drummer to beat the morning drum.

DIRGE FOR TWO VETERANS.

1.

The last sunbeam
Lightly falls from the finished Sabbath
On the pavement here—and, there beyond, it is looking
    Down a new-made double grave.

2.

Lo! the moon ascending!
Up from the east, the silvery round moon;
Beautiful over the house-tops, ghastly, phantom moon;
    Immense and silent moon.

3.

I see a sad procession,
And I hear the sound of coming full-keyed bugles;
All the channels of the city streets they're flooding,
    As with voices and with tears.

4.

I hear the great drums pounding,
And the small drums steady whirring;
And every blow of the great convulsive drums
    Strikes me through and through.

5.

For the son is brought with the father;
In the foremost ranks of the fierce assault they fell;
Two veterans, son and father, dropped together,
  And the double grave awaits them.

6.

Now nearer blow the bugles,
And the drums strike more convulsive;
And the daylight o'er the pavement quite has faded,
  And the strong dead-march enwraps me.

7.

In the eastern sky up-buoying,
The sorrowful vast phantom moves illumined,
'Tis some mother's large, transparent face,
  In heaven brighter growing.

8.

O strong dead-march, you please me!
O moon immense, with your silvery face you soothe me!
O my soldiers twain! O my veterans, passing to burial!
  What I have I also give you.

9.

The moon gives you light,
And the bugles and the drums give you music;
And my heart, O my soldiers, my veterans,
  My heart gives you love.

SURVIVORS.

How solemn, as one by one,
As the ranks returning, all worn and sweaty—as the men
    file by where I stand;
As the faces, the masks appear—as I glance at the faces,
    studying the masks;
As I glance upward out of this page, studying you, dear
    friend, whoever you are;—
How solemn the thought of my whispering soul, to each
    in the ranks, and to you!
I see, behind each mask, that wonder, a kindred soul.
O the bullet could never kill what you really are, dear
    friend,
Nor the bayonet stab what you really are.
—The soul, yourself, I see, great as any, good as the best,
Waiting secure and content,—which the bullet could
    never kill,
Nor the bayonet stab, O friend!

HYMN OF DEAD SOLDIERS.

1.

One breath, O my silent soul!
A perfumed thought—no more I ask, for the sake of all
    dead soldiers.

2.

Buglers off in my armies!
At present I ask not you to sound;
Not at the head of my cavalry, all on their spirited horses,
With their sabres drawn and glistening, and carbines
    clanking by their thighs—(ah, my brave horsemen!
My handsome, tan-faced horsemen! what life, what joy
    and pride,
With all the perils, were yours!)

Nor you drummers—neither at *reveillé*, at dawn,
Nor the long roll alarming the camp—nor even the
    muffled beat for a burial;
Nothing from you, this time, O drummers, bearing my
    warlike drums.

3.

But aside from these, and the crowd's hurrahs, and the
    land's congratulations,
Admitting around me comrades close, unseen by the rest,
    and voiceless,

I chant this chant of my silent soul, in the name of all
  dead soldiers.

4.

Faces so pale, with wondrous eyes, very dear, gather closer
    yet;
Draw close, but speak not.
Phantoms, welcome, divine and tender!
Invisible to the rest, henceforth become my companions;
Follow me ever! desert me not, while I live!

Sweet are the blooming cheeks of the living, sweet are the
    musical voices sounding;
But sweet, ah sweet, are the dead, with their silent eyes.

Dearest comrades! all now is over;
But love is not over—and what love, O comrades!
Perfume from battlefields rising—up from foetor arising.

Perfume therefore my chant, O love! immortal love!
Give me to bathe the memories of all dead soldiers.

Perfume all! make all wholesome!
O love! O chant! solve all with the last chemistry.

Give me exhaustless—make me a fountain,
That I exhale love from me wherever I go,
For the sake of all dead soldiers.

SPIRIT WHOSE WORK IS DONE.

Spirit whose work is done! spirit of dreadful hours!
Ere, departing, fade from my eyes your forests of
    bayonets—
Spirit of gloomiest fears and doubts, yet onward ever
    unfaltering pressing!
Spirit of many a solemn day, and many a savage scene!
    Electric spirit!
That with muttering voice, through the years now closed,
    like a tireless phantom flitted,
Rousing the land with breath of flame, while you beat and
    beat the drum;
—Now, as the sound of the drum, hollow and harsh to the
    last, reverberates round me;
As your ranks, your immortal ranks, return, return from
    the battles;
While the muskets of the young men yet lean over their
    shoulders;
While I look on the bayonets bristling over their
    shoulders;
While those slanted bayonets, whole forests of them,
    appearing in the distance, approach and pass on,
    returning homeward,
Moving with steady motion, swaying to and fro, to the
    right and left,
Evenly, lightly, rising and falling, as the steps keep time:
—Spirit of hours I knew, all hectic red one day, but pale as
    death next day;
Touch my mouth, ere you depart—press my lips close!

Leave me your pulses of rage! bequeath them to me! fill
    me with currents convulsive!
Let them scorch and blister out of my chants, when you
    are gone;
Let them identify you to the future in these songs!

RECONCILIATION.

Word over all, beautiful as the sky!
Beautiful that war, and all its deeds of carnage, must in
time be utterly lost;
That the hands of the sisters Death and Night incessantly,
softly wash again, and ever again, this soiled world.
For my enemy is dead—a man divine as myself is dead.
I look where he lies, white-faced and still, in the coffin—I
draw near;
I bend down and touch lightly with my lips the white face
in the coffin.

AFTER THE WAR.

To the leavened soil they trod, calling, I sing, for the last;
Not cities, nor man alone, nor war, nor the dead:
But forth from my tent emerging for good—loosing,
    untying the tent-ropes;
In the freshness, the forenoon air, in the far-stretching
    circuits and vistas, again to peace restored;
To the fiery fields emanative, and the endless vistas
    beyond—to the south and the north;
To the leavened soil of the general Western World, to
    attest my songs,
To the average earth, the wordless earth, witness of war
    and peace,
To the Alleghanian hills, and the tireless Mississippi,
To the rocks I, calling, sing, and all the trees in the woods,
To the plain of the poems of heroes, to the prairie
    spreading wide,
To the far-off sea, and the unseen winds, and the sane
    impalpable air.
And responding they answer all, (but not in words,)
The average earth, the witness of war and peace,
    acknowledges mutely;
The prairie draws me close, as the father, to bosom broad,
    the son:—
The Northern ice and rain, that began me, nourish me to
    the end;
But the hot sun of the South is to ripen my songs.

WALT WHITMAN

ASSIMILATIONS.

1.

There was a child went forth every day;
And the first object he looked upon, that object he
    became;
And that object became part of him for the day, or
    a certain part of the day, or for many years, or
    stretching cycles of years.

2.

The early lilacs became part of this child,
And grass, and white and red morning-glories,[1] and
    white and red clover, and the song of the phoebe-
    bird,[2]
And the Third-month lambs, and the sow's pink-faint
    litter, and the mare's foal, and the cow's calf,
And the noisy brood of the barn-yard, or by the mire of
    the pond-side,
And the fish suspending themselves so curiously below
    there—and the beautiful, curious liquid,
And the water-plants with their graceful fiat heads—all
    became part of him.

The field-sprouts of Fourth-month and Fifth-month
    became part or him;

Winter-grain sprouts, and those of the light-yellow corn,
    and the esculent roots of the garden,

And the apple-trees covered with blossoms, and the fruit
    afterward, and wood-berries, and the commonest
    weeds by the road;
And the old drunkard staggering home from the
    outhouse of the tavern, whence he had lately risen,
And the schoolmistress that passed on her way to the
    school,
And the friendly boys that passed, and the quarrelsome
    boys,
And the tidy and fresh-cheeked girls, and the barefoot
    negro boy and girl,
And all the changes of city and country, wherever he
    went.

His own parents;
He that had fathered him, and she that had conceived him
    in her womb, and birthed him,
They gave this child more of themselves than that;
They gave him afterward every day—they became part of
    him.
The mother at home, quietly placing the dishes on the
    supper-table;
The mother with mild words—clean her cap and gown, a
    wholesome odour falling off her person and clothes as
    she walks by;
The father, strong, self-sufficient, manly, mean, angered,
    unjust;
The blow, the quick loud word, the tight bargain, the
    crafty lure,
The family usages, the language, the company, the
    furniture—the yearning and swelling heart,
Affection that will not be gainsaid—the sense of what is
    real—the thought if after all it should prove unreal,
The doubts of day-time and the doubts of night-time—the
    curious whether and how—

Whether that which appears so is so, or is it all flashes
   and specks?
Men and women crowding fast in the streets—if they are
   not flashes and specks, what are they?
The streets themselves, and the façades of houses, and
   goods in the windows,
Vehicles, teams, the heavy-planked wharves—the huge
   crossing at the ferries,
The village on the highland, seen from afar at sunset—the
   river between;
Shadows, aureola and mist, light falling on roofs and
   gables of white or brown, three miles off;
The schooner near by, sleepily dropping down the tide—
   the little boat slack-towed astern,
The hurrying tumbling waves quick-broken crests
   slapping,
The strata of coloured clouds, the long bar of maroon-
   tint, away solitary by itself-the spread of purity it lies
   motionless in,
The horizon's edge, the flying sea-crow, the fragrance of
   salt marsh and shore mud;—
These became part of that child who went forth every day,
   and who now goes, and will always go forth every day.

FOOTNOTES :

1. *The name of "morning-glory" is given to the bindweed, or a sort of*
   bindweed, in America. I am not certain whether this expressive
   name is used in England also.
2. *A dun-coloured little bird with a cheerful note, sounding like the*
   word Phoebe.

A WORD OUT OF THE SEA.

1.

Out of the rocked cradle,
Out of the mocking-bird's throat, the musical shuttle,
Out of the Ninth-month midnight,
Over the sterile sands, and the fields beyond, where the
    child, leaving his bed, wandered alone, bareheaded,
    barefoot,
Down from the showered halo,
Up from the mystic play of shadows, twining and
    twisting; as if they were alive,
Out from the patches of briars and blackberries,
From the memories of the birds that chanted to me,
From your memories, sad brother—from the fitful risings
    and fallings I heard,
From under that yellow half-moon, late-risen, and swollen
    as if with tears,
From those beginning notes of sickness and love, there in
    the transparent mist,
From the thousand responses of my heart, never to cease,
From the myriad thence-aroused words,
From the word stronger and more delicious than any,—
From such, as now they start, the scene revisiting,
As a flock, twittering, rising, or overhead passing,
Borne hither—ere all eludes me, hurriedly,—
A man—yet by these tears a little boy again,
Throwing myself on the sand, confronting the waves,
I, chanter of pains and joys, uniter of here and hereafter,

Taking all hints to use them, but swiftly leaping beyond
    them,
A reminiscence sing.

2.

Once, Paumanok,
When the snows had melted, and the Fifth-month grass
    was growing,
Up this sea-shore, in some briars,
Two guests from Alabama—two together,
And their nest, and four light-green eggs spotted with
    brown;
And every day the he-bird, to and fro, near at hand,
And every day the she-bird, crouched on her nest, silent,
    with bright eyes;
And every day I, a curious boy, never too close, never
    disturbing them,
Cautiously peering, absorbing, translating.

3.

Shine! shine! shine!
Pour down your warmth, great Sun!
While we bask—we two together.

Two together!
Winds blow South, or winds blow North,
Day come white or night come black,
Home, or rivers and mountains from home,
Singing all time, minding no time,
If we two but keep together.

4.

Till of a sudden,
Maybe killed, unknown to her mate,
One forenoon the she-bird crouched not on the nest,
Nor returned that afternoon, nor the next,
Nor ever appeared again.

And thenceforward, all summer, in the sound of the sea,
And at night, under the full of the moon, in calmer
    weather,
Over the hoarse surging of the sea,
Or flitting from briar to briar by day,
I saw, I heard at intervals, the remaining one, the he-bird,
The solitary guest from Alabama.

5.

Blow! blow! blow!
Blow up, sea-winds, along Paumanok's shore!
I wait and I wait, till you blow my mate to me.

6.

Yes, when the stars glistened.
All night long, on the prong of a moss-scalloped stake,
Down, almost amid the slapping waves,
Sat the lone singer, wonderful, causing tears.

He called on his mate;
He poured forth the meanings which I, of all men, know.
Yes, my brother, I know;
The rest might not—but I have treasured every note;
For once, and more than once, dimly, down to the beach
    gliding,

Silent, avoiding the moonbeams, blending myself with the
    shadows,
Recalling now the obscure shapes, the echoes, the sounds
    and sights after their sorts,
The white arms out in the breakers tirelessly tossing,
I, with bare feet, a child, the wind wafting my hair,
Listened long and long.

Listened, to keep, to sing—now translating the notes,
Following you, my brother.

7.

Soothe! soothe! soothe!
Close on its wave soothes the wave behind,
And again another behind, embracing and lapping, every
    one close,—
But my love soothes not me, not me.

Low hangs the moon—it rose late;
O it is lagging—O I think it is heavy with love, with love.

O madly the sea pushes, pushes upon the land,
With love—with love.

O night! do I not see my love fluttering out there among the
    breakers?
What is that little black thing I see there in the white?

Loud! loud! loud!
Loud. I call to you, my love!
High and clear I shoot my voice over the waves;
Surely you must know who is here, is here;
You must know who I am, my love.

Low-hanging moon!
What is that dusky spot in your brown yellow?
O it is the shape, the shape of my mate!
O moon, do not keep her from me any longer!

Land! land! O land!
Whichever way I turn, O I think you could give me my
    mate back again, if you only would;
For I am almost sure I see her dimly whichever way I look.

O rising stars!
Perhaps the one I want so much will rise, will rise with
    some of you.

O throat! O trembling throat!
Sound clearer through the atmosphere!
Pierce the woods, the earth;
Somewhere, listening to catch you, must be the one I want.

Shake out, carols!
Solitary here—the night's carols!
Carols of lonesome love! Death's carols!
Carols under that lagging, yellow, waning moon!
O, under that moon, where she droops almost down into
    the sea!
O reckless, despairing carols!

But soft! sink low;
Soft! let me just murmur;
And do you wait a moment, you husky-noised sea;
For somewhere I believe I heard my mate responding to me,
So faint—I must be still, be still to listen;
But not altogether still, for then she might not come
    immediately to me.

Hither, my love!
Here I am! Here!
With this just-sustained note I announce myself to you;
This gentle call is for you, my love, for you!

Do not be decoyed elsewhere!
That is the whistle of the wind—it is not my voice;
That is the fluttering, the flattering of the spray;
Those are the shadows of leaves.

O darkness! O in vain!
O I am very sick and sorrowful!
O brown halo in the sky, near the moon, drooping upon the
    sea!
O troubled reflection in the sea!
O throat! O throbbing heart!
O all!—and I singing uselessly, uselessly all the night.!

Yet I murmur, murmur on!
O murmurs—you yourselves make me continue to sing, I
    know not why.

O past! O life! O songs of joy!
In the air—in the woods—over fields;
Loved! loved! loved! loved! loved!
But my love no more, no more with me!
We two together no more!

8.

The aria sinking;
All else continuing—the stars shining,
The winds blowing—the notes of the bird continuous
    echoing,

With angry moans the fierce old Mother incessantly
    moaning,
On the sands of Paumanok's shore, grey and rustling;
The yellow half-moon enlarged, sagging down, drooping,
    the face of the sea almost touching;
The boy ecstatic—with his bare feet the waves, with his
    hair the atmosphere, dallying,
The love in the heart long pent, now loose, now at last
    tumultuously bursting;
The aria's meaning the ears, the soul, swiftly depositing,
The strange tears down the cheeks coursing;
The colloquy there—the trio—each uttering;
The undertone—the savage old Mother, incessantly
    crying,
To the boy's soul's questions sullenly timing—some
    drowned secret hissing
To the outsetting bard of love.

9.

Demon or bird! (said the boy's soul,)
Is it indeed toward your mate you sing? or is it mostly to
    me?
For I, that was a child, my tongue's use sleeping,
Now I have heard you,
Now in a moment I know what I am for—I awake;
And already a thousand singers—a thousand songs,
    clearer, louder, and more sorrowful than yours,
A thousand warbling echoes, have started to life within
    me,
Never to die.

O you singer, solitary, singing by yourself—projecting me;
O solitary me, listening—never more shall I cease
    perpetuating you;

Never more shall I escape, never more, the reverberations,
Never more the cries of unsatisfied love be absent from
    me,
Never again leave me to be the peaceful child I was before
    what there, in the night,
By the sea, under the yellow and sagging moon,
The messenger there aroused—the fire, the sweet hell
    within,
The unknown want, the destiny of me.

O give me the clue! (it lurks in the night here somewhere;)
O if I am to have so much, let me have more!
O a word! O what is my destination? I fear it is henceforth
    chaos;—
O how joys, dreads, convolutions, human shapes and all
    shapes, spring as from graves around me!
O phantoms! you cover all the land, and all the sea!
O I cannot see in the dimness whether you smile or frown
    upon me;
O vapour, a look, a word! O well-beloved!
O you dear women's and men's phantoms!

A word then, (for I will conquer it,)
The word final, superior to all,
Subtle, sent up—what is it?—I listen;
Are you whispering it, and have been all the time, you
    sea-waves?
Is that it from your liquid rims and wet sands?

10.

Whereto answering, the Sea,
Delaying not, hurrying not,
Whispered me through the night, and very plainly before
    daybreak,

Lisped to me the low and delicious word DEATH;
And again Death—ever Death, Death, Death,
Hissing melodious, neither like the bird nor like my
    aroused child's heart,
But edging near, as privately for me, rustling at my feet,
Creeping thence steadily up to my ears, and laving me
    softly all over,
Death, Death, Death, Death, Death.

Which I do not forget,
But fuse the song of my dusky demon and brother,
That he sang to me in the moonlight on Paumanok's grey
    beach,
With the thousand responsive songs, at random,
My own songs, awaked from that hour;
And with them the key, the word up from the waves,
The word of the sweetest song, and all songs,
That strong and delicious word which, creeping to my
    feet,
The Sea whispered me.

CROSSING BROOKLYN FERRY.

1.

Flood-tide below me! I watch you face to face;
Clouds of the west! sun there half an hour high! I see you
    also face to face.

2.

Crowds of men and women attired in the usual costumes,
    how curious you are to me!
On the ferry-boats the hundreds and hundreds that cross,
    returning home, are more curious to me than you
    suppose;
And you that shall cross from shore to shore years hence
    are more to me, and more in my meditations, than
    you might suppose.

3.

The impalpable sustenance of me from all things, at all
    hours of the day;
The simple, compact, well-joined scheme—myself
    disintegrated, every one disintegrated, yet part of the
    scheme;
The similitudes of the past, and those of the future;
The glories strung like beads on my smallest sights and
    hearings—on the walk in the street, and the passage
    over the river;

The current rushing so swiftly, and swimming with me
　　far away;
The others that are to follow me, the ties between me and
　　them;
The certainty of others—the life, love, sight, hearing, of
　　others.

Others will enter the gates of the ferry, and cross from
　　shore to shore;
Others will watch the run of the flood-tide;
Others will see the shipping of Manhattan north and
　　west, and the heights of Brooklyn to the south and
　　east;
Others will see the islands large and small;
Fifty years hence, others will see them as they cross, the
　　sun half an hour high;

A hundred years hence, or ever so many hundred years
　　hence, others will see them,
Will enjoy the sunset, the pouring-in of the flood-tide, the
　　falling-back to the sea of the ebb-tide.

It avails not, neither time nor place—distance avails not;
I am with you—you men and women of a generation, or
　　ever so many generations hence;
I project myself—also I return—I am with you, and know
　　how it is.

Just as you feel when you look on the river and sky, so I
　　felt;
Just as any of you is one of a living crowd, I was one of a
　　crowd;
Just as you are refreshed by the gladness of the river and
　　the bright flow,
I was refreshed;

Just as you stand and lean on the rail, yet hurry with the
    swift current, I stood, yet was hurried;
Just as you look on the numberless masts of ships, and the
    thick-stemmed pipes of steamboats, I looked.

I too many and many a time crossed the river, the sun
    half an hour high;
I watched the twelfth-month sea-gulls—I saw them high
    in the air, floating with motionless wings, oscillating
    their bodies,
I saw how the glistening yellow lit up parts of their bodies,
    and left the rest in strong shadow,
I saw the slow-wheeling circles, and the gradual edging
    toward the south.

I too saw the reflection of the summer sky in the water,
Had my eyes dazzled by the shimmering track of beams,
Looked at the fine centrifugal spokes of light round the
    shape of my head in the sun-lit water,
Looked on the haze on the hills southward and
    southwestward,
Looked on the vapour as it flew in fleeces tinged with
    violet,
Looked toward the lower bay to notice the arriving ships,
Saw their approach, saw aboard those that were near me,
Saw the white sails of schooners and sloops, saw the ships
    at anchor,
The sailors at work in the rigging, or out astride the spars.
The round masts, the swinging motion of the hulls, the
    slender serpentine pennants,
The large and small steamers in motion, the pilots in their
    pilot-houses,
The white wake left by the passage, the quick tremulous
    whirl of the wheels,
The flags of all nations, the falling of them at sunset,

The scallop-edged waves in the twilight, the ladled cups,
    the frolicsome crests and glistening,
The stretch afar growing dimmer and dimmer, the grey
    walls of the granite store-houses by the docks,
On the river the shadowy group, the big steam-tug closely
    flanked on each side by the barges—the hay-boat, the
    belated lighter,
On the neighbouring shore, the fires from the foundry
    chimneys burning high and glaringly into the night,
Casting their flicker of black, contrasted with wild red
    and yellow light, over the tops of houses and down
    into the clefts of streets.

These, and all else, were to me the same as they are to you;
I project myself a moment to tell you—also I return.

I loved well those cities;
I loved well the stately and rapid river;
The men and women I saw were all near to me;
Others the same—others who look back on me because I
    looked forward to them;
The time will come, though I stop here to-day and to-
    night.

What is it, then, between us?
What is the count of the scores or hundreds of years
    between us?

Whatever it is, it avails not—distance avails not, and place
    avails not.

I too lived—Brooklyn, of ample hills, was mine;
I too walked the streets of Manhattan Island, and bathed
    in the waters around it;
I too felt the curious abrupt questionings stir within me;

In the day, among crowds of people, sometimes they came
    upon me,
In my walks home late at night, or as I lay in my bed, they
    came upon me.

I too had been struck from the float for ever held in
    solution, I too had received identity by my Body;
That I was, I knew, was of my body—and what I should
    be, I knew, I should be of my body.

It is not upon you alone the dark patches fall,
The dark threw patches down upon me also;
The best I had done seemed to me blank and suspicious;
My great thoughts, as I supposed them, were they not in
    reality meagre? would not people laugh at me?
It is not you alone who know what it is to be evil;
I am he who knew what it was to be evil;
I too knitted the old knot of contrariety,
Blabbed, blushed, resented, lied, stole, grudged;
Had guile, anger, lust, hot wishes I dared not speak;
Was wayward, vain, greedy, shallow, sly, cowardly,
    malignant;
The wolf, the snake, the hog, not wanting in me;
The cheating look, the frivolous word, the adulterous
    wish, not wanting;
Refusals, hates, postponements, meanness, laziness, none
    of these wanting.

But I was Manhattanese, friendly and proud!
I was called by my nighest name by clear loud voices of
    young men as they saw me approaching or passing,
Felt their arms on my neck as I stood, or the negligent
    leaning of their flesh against me as I sat;
Saw many I loved in the street, or ferry-boat, or public
    assembly, yet never told them a word;

Lived the same life with the rest, the same old laughing,
    gnawing, sleeping;
Played the part that still looks back on the actor or
    actress,
The same old rôle, the rôle that is what we make it,—as
    great as we like,
Or as small as we like, or both great and small.

Closer yet I approach you:
What thought you have of me, I had as much of you— I
    laid in my stores in advance;
I considered long and seriously of you before you were
    born.

Who was to know what should come home to me?
Who knows but I am enjoying this?
Who knows but I am as good as looking at you now, for
    all you cannot see me?

It is not you alone, nor I alone;
Not a few races, nor a few generations, nor a few
    centuries;
It is that each came or comes or shall come from its due
emission, without fail, either now or then or henceforth.

Everything indicates—the smallest does, and the largest
    does;
A necessary film envelops all, and envelops the Soul for a
    proper time.

Now I am curious what sight can ever be more stately and
    admirable to me than my mast-hemmed Manhatta,
My river and sunset, and my scallop-edged waves of
    flood-tide;

The sea-gulls oscillating their bodies, the hay-boat in the
    twilight, and the belated lighter;
Curious what Gods can exceed these that clasp me by the
    hand, and with voices I love call me promptly and
    loudly by my nighest name as I approach;
Curious what is more subtle than this which ties me to
    the woman or man that looks in my face,
Which fuses me into you now, and pours my meaning
    into you.

We understand, then, do we not?
What I promised without mentioning it have you not
    accepted?
What the study could not teach—what the preaching
    could not accomplish, is accomplished, is it not?
What the push of reading could not start, is started by me
    personally, is it not?

4.

Flow on river! flow with the flood-tide, and ebb with the
    ebb-tide!
Frolic on, crested and scallop-edged waves!
Gorgeous clouds of the sunset, drench with your
    splendour me, or the men and women generations
    after me!
Cross from shore to shore, countless crowds of
    passengers!
Stand up, tall masts of Mannahatta!-stand up, beautiful
    hills of Brooklyn!
Bully for you! you proud, friendly, free Manhattanese!
Throb, baffled and curious brain! throw out questions and
    answers!
Suspend here and everywhere, eternal float of solution!
Blab, blush, lie, steal, you or I or any one after us!

Gaze, loving and thirsting eyes, in the house, or street, or
    public assembly!
Sound out, voices of young men! loudly and musically call
    me by my nighest name!
Live, old life! play the part that looks back on the actor or
    actress!
Play the old role, the role that is great or small, according
    as one makes it!
Consider, you who peruse me, whether I may not in
    unknown ways be looking upon you:
Be firm, rail over the river, to support those who lean idly,
    yet haste with the hasting current;
Fly on, sea-birds! fly sideways, or wheel in large circles
    high in the air;
Receive the summer sky, you water! and faithfully hold it,
    till all downcast eyes have time to take it from you;
Diverge, fine spokes of light, from the shape of my head,
    or any one's head, in the sun-lit water;
Come on, ships from the lower bay! pass up or down,
    white-sailed schooners, sloops, lighters!
Flaunt away, flags of all nations! be duly lowered at sunset;
Burn high your fires, foundry chimneys! cast black
    shadows at nightfall; cast red and yellow light over the
    tops of the houses;
Appearances, now or henceforth, indicate what you are;
You necessary film, continue to envelop the soul;
About my body for me, and your body for you, be hung
    our divinest aromas;
Thrive, cities! bring your freight, bring your shows, ample
    and sufficient rivers!
Expand, being than which none else is perhaps more
    spiritual!
Keep your places, objects than which none else is more
    lasting!

We descend upon you and all things—we arrest you all;
We realise the soul only by you, you faithful solids and
    fluids;
Through you colour, form, location, sublimity, ideality;
Through you every proof, comparison, and all the
    suggestions and determinations of ourselves.

You have waited, you always wait, you dumb, beautiful
    ministers! you novices!
We receive you with free sense at last, and are insatiate
    henceforward;
Not you any more shall be able to foil us, or withhold
    yourselves from us;
We use you, and do not cast you aside—we plant you
    permanently within us;
We fathom you not—we love you—there is perfection in
    you also;
You furnish your parts toward eternity;
Great or small, you furnish your parts toward the soul.

NIGHT AND DEATH.

1.

Night on the prairies.
The supper is over—the fire on the ground burns low;
The wearied emigrants sleep, wrapped in their blankets;
I walk by myself—I stand and look at the stars, which I
    think now I never realised before.

Now I absorb immortality and peace,
I admire death, and test propositions.

How plenteous! How spiritual! How *resumé*!
The same Old Man and Soul—the same old aspirations,
    and the same content.

2.

I was thinking the day most splendid, till I saw what the
    not day exhibited,
I was thinking this globe enough, till there sprang out so
    noiseless around me myriads of other globes.

Now, while the great thoughts of space and eternity fill
    me, I will measure myself by them:
And now, touched with the lives of other globes, arrived
    as far along as those of the earth,
Or waiting to arrive, or passed on farther than those of
    the earth,

I henceforth no more ignore them than I ignore my own
　　life,
Or the lives of the earth arrived as far as mine, or waiting
　　to arrive.

3.

O I see now that life cannot exhibit all to me-as the day
　　cannot,
I see that I am to wait for what will be exhibited by death.

ELEMENTAL DRIFTS.

1.

Elemental drifts!
O I wish I could impress others as you and the waves have
　　just been impressing me.

As I ebbed with an ebb of the ocean of life,
As I wended the shores I know,
As I walked where the sea-ripples wash you, Paumanok,
Where they rustle up, hoarse and sibilant,
Where the fierce old Mother endlessly cries for her
　　castaways,
I, musing, late in the autumn day, gazing off southward,
Alone, held by this eternal self of me, out of the pride of
　　which I have uttered my poems,
Was seized by the spirit that trails in the lines underfoot,
In the rim, the sediment, that stands for all the water and
　　all the land of the globe.

Fascinated, my eyes, reverting from the south, dropped,
　　to follow those slender winrows,
Chaff, straw, splinters of wood, weeds, and the sea-gluten,
Scum, scales from shining rocks, leaves of salt-lettuce, left
　　by the tide;
Miles walking, the sound of breaking waves the other side
　　of me,
Paumanok, there and then, as I thought the old thought
　　of likenesses.
These you presented to me, you fish-shaped Island,

As I wended the shores I know,
As I walked with that eternal self of me, seeking types.

2.

As I wend to the shores I know not,
As I list to the dirge, the voices of men and women
    wrecked,
As I inhale the impalpable breezes that set in upon me,
As the ocean so mysterious rolls toward me closer and
    closer,
I too but signify, at the utmost, a little washed-up drift,
A few sands and dead leaves to gather,
Gather, and merge myself as part of the sands and drift.
O baffled, baulked, bent to the very earth,
Oppressed with myself that I have dared to open my
    mouth,
Aware now that, amid all the blab whose echoes recoil
    upon me, I have not once had the least idea who or
    what I am,
But that before all my insolent poems, the real ME stands
    yet untouched, untold, altogether unreached,
Withdrawn far, mocking me with mock-congratulatory
    signs and bows,
With peals of distant ironical laughter at every word I
    have written,
Pointing in silence to all these songs, and then to the sand
    beneath.

Now I perceive I have not understood anything—not a
    single object—and that no man ever can.

I perceive Nature, here in sight of the sea, is taking
    advantage of me, to dart upon me, and sting me,
Because I have dared to open my mouth to sing at all.

3.

You oceans both! I close with you;
These little shreds shall indeed stand for all.

You friable shore, with trails of debris!
You fish-shaped Island! I take what is underfoot;
What is yours is mine, my father.

I too, Paumanok,
I too have bubbled up, floated the measureless float, and
    been washed on your shores;
I too am but a trail of drift and debris,
I too leave little wrecks upon you, you fish-shaped Island.

I throw myself upon your breast, my father,
I cling to you so that you cannot unloose me,
I hold you so firm till you answer me something.

Kiss me, my father,
Touch me with your lips, as I touch those I love,
Breathe to me, while I hold you close, the secret of the
    wondrous murmuring I envy.

4.

Ebb, ocean of life, (the flow will return.)
Cease not your moaning, you fierce old Mother,
Endlessly cry for your castaways—but fear not, deny not
    me,
Rustle not up so hoarse and angry against my feet, as I
    touch you, or gather from you.

I mean tenderly by you,

I gather for myself, and for this phantom, looking down
    where we lead, and following me and mine.

Me and mine!
We, loose winrows, little corpses,
Froth, snowy white, and bubbles,
(See! from my dead lips the ooze exuding at last!
See—the prismatic colours, glistening and rolling!)
Tufts of straw, sands, fragments,
Buoyed hither from many moods, one contradicting
    another,
From the storm, the long calm, the darkness, the swell;
Musing, pondering, a breath, a briny tear, a dab of liquid
    or soil;
Up just as much out of fathomless workings fermented
    and thrown;
A limp blossom or two, torn, just as much over waves
    floating, drifted at random;
Just as much for us that sobbing dirge of Nature;
Just as much, whence we come, that blare of the cloud-
    trumpets;
We, capricious, brought hither, we know not whence,
    spread out before you,
You, up there, walking or sitting,
Whoever you are—we too lie in drifts at your feet.

WONDERS.

1.

Who learns my lesson complete?
Boss, journeyman, apprentice—churchman and atheist,
The stupid and the wise thinker—parents and offspring—
    merchant, clerk, porter, and customer,
Editor, author, artist; and schoolboy—Draw nigh and
    commence;
It is no lesson—it lets down the bars to a good lesson,
And that to another, and every one to another still.

2.

The great laws take and effuse without argument;
I am of the same style, for I am their friend,
I love them quits and quits—I do not halt and make
    salaams.

I lie abstracted, and hear beautiful tales of things, and the
    reasons of things;
They are so beautiful I nudge myself to listen.
I cannot say to any person what I hear—I cannot say it to
    myself—it is very wonderful.

It is no small matter, this round and delicious globe,
    moving so exactly in its orbit for ever and ever,
    without one jolt, or the untruth of a single second;
I do not think it was made in six days, nor in ten
    thousand years, nor ten billions of years,

Nor planned and built one thing after another, as an
   architect plans and builds a house.
I do not think seventy years is the time of a man or
   woman,
Nor that seventy millions of years is the time of a man or
   woman,
Nor that years will ever stop the existence of me, or any
   one else.

3.

Is it wonderful that I should be immortal? as every one is
   immortal;
I know it is wonderful—but my eyesight is equally
   wonderful, and how I was conceived in my mother's
   womb is equally wonderful;
And passed from a babe, in the creeping trance of a
   couple of summers and winters, to articulate and
   walk—All this is equally wonderful.

And that my Soul embraces you this hour, and we affect
   each other without ever seeing each other, and never
   perhaps to see each other, is every bit as wonderful.

And that I can think such thoughts as these is just as
   wonderful;
And that I can remind you, and you think them and
   know them to be true, is just as wonderful.
And that the moon spins round the earth, and on with
   the earth, is equally wonderful;
And that they balance themselves with the sun and stars
   is equally wonderful.

MIRACLES.

1.

What shall I give? and which are my miracles?

2.

Realism is mine—my miracles—Take freely,
Take without end—I offer them to you wherever your feet
   can carry you or your eyes reach.

3.

Why! who makes much of a miracle?
As to me, I know of nothing else but miracles,
Whether I walk the streets of Manhattan,
Or dart my sight over the roofs of houses toward the sky,
Or wade with naked feet along the beach, just in the edge
   of the water,
Or stand under trees in the woods,
Or talk by day with any one I love—or sleep in the bed at
   night with any one I love,
Or sit at the table at dinner with my mother,
Or look at strangers opposite me riding in the car,
Or watch honey-bees busy around the hive, of a summer
   forenoon,
Or animals feeding in the fields,
Or birds—or the wonderfulness of insects in the air,
Or the wonderfulness of the sundown—or of stars
   shining so quiet and bright,

Or the exquisite, delicate, thin curve of the new moon in
    spring;
Or whether I go among those I like best, and that like me
    best—mechanics, boatmen, farmers,
Or among the savans—or to the *soirée*—or to the opera.
Or stand a long while looking at the movements of
    machinery,
Or behold children at their sports,
Or the admirable sight of the perfect old man, or the
    perfect old woman,
Or the sick in hospitals, or the dead carried to burial,
Or my own eyes and figure in the glass;
These, with the rest, one and all, are to me miracles,
The whole referring—yet each distinct and in its place.

4.

To me, every hour of the light and dark is a miracle,
Every inch of space is a miracle,
Every square yard of the surface of the earth is spread
    with the same,
Every cubic foot of the interior swarms with the same;
Every spear of grass—the frames, limbs, organs, of men
    and women, and all that concerns them,
All these to me are unspeakably perfect miracles.

To me the sea is a continual miracle;
The fishes that swim—the rocks—the motion of the
    waves—the ships, with men in them,
What stranger miracles are there?

VISAGES.

Of the visages of things—And of piercing through to the
   accepted hells beneath.
Of ugliness—To me there is just as much in it as there is
   in beauty—And now the ugliness of human beings is
   acceptable to me.
Of detected persons—To me, detected persons are not, in
   any respect, worse than undetected persons—and are
   not in any respect worse than I am myself.
Of criminals—To me, any judge, or any juror, is equally
   criminal—and any reputable person is also—and the
   President is also.

THE DARK SIDE.

I sit and look out upon all the sorrows of the world, and
upon all oppression and shame;
I hear secret convulsive sobs from young men, at anguish
with themselves, remorseful after deeds done;
I see, in low life, the mother misused by her children,
dying, neglected, gaunt, desperate;
I see the wife misused by her husband—I see the
treacherous seducer of young women;
I mark the ranklings of jealousy and unrequited love,
attempted to be hid— I see these sights on the earth;
I see the workings of battle, pestilence, tyranny—I see
martyrs and prisoners;
I observe a famine at sea—I observe the sailors casting
lots who shall be killed, to preserve the lives of the
rest;
I observe the slights and degradations cast by arrogant
persons upon labourers, the poor, and upon negroes,
and the like;
All these—all the meanness and agony without end, I,
sitting, look out upon;
See, hear, and am silent.

MUSIC.

I heard you, solemn-sweet pipes of the organ, as last
 Sunday morn I passed the church;
Winds of autumn!—as I walked the woods at dusk,
 I heard your long-stretched sighs, up above, so
 mournful;
I heard the perfect Italian tenor, singing at the opera—I
 heard the soprano in the midst of the quartette
 singing.
....Heart of my love! you too I heard, murmuring low,
 through one of the wrists around my head;
Heard the pulse of you, when all was still, ringing little
 bells last night under my ear.

WHEREFORE?

O me! O life!—of the questions of these recurring;
Of the endless trains of the faithless—of cities filled with
    the foolish;
Of myself for ever reproaching myself, (for who more
    foolish than I, and who more faithless?)
Of eyes that vainly crave the light—of the objects mean—
    of the struggle ever renewed;
Of the poor results of all—of the plodding and sordid
    crowds I see around me;
Of the empty and useless years of the rest—with the rest
    me intertwined;
The question, O me! so sad, recurring—What good amid
    these, O me, O life?

Answer.

That you are here—that life exists, and identity;
That the powerful play goes on, and you will contribute a
    verse.

QUESTIONABLE.

As I lay with my head in your lap, camerado,
The confession I made I resume—what I said to you and
the open air I resume.
I know I am restless, and make others so;
I know my words are weapons, full of danger, full of
death;
(Indeed I am myself the real soldier;
It is not he, there, with his bayonet, and not the red-
striped artilleryman;)
For I confront peace, security, and all the settled laws, to
unsettle them;
I am more resolute because all have denied me than I
could ever have been had all accepted me;
I heed not, and have never heeded, either experience,
cautions, majorities, nor ridicule;
And the threat of what is called hell is little or nothing to
me;
And the lure of what is called heaven is little or nothing
to me.
...Dear camerado! I confess I have urged you onward with
me, and still urge you, without the least idea what is
our destination,
Or whether we shall be victorious, or utterly quelled and
defeated.

POEMS BY WALT WHITMAN

SONG AT SUNSET.

1.

Splendour of ended day, floating and filling me!
Hour prophetic—hour resuming the past:
Inflating my throat—you, divine Average!
You, Earth and Life, till the last ray gleams, I sing.

2.

Open mouth of my soul, uttering gladness,
Eyes of my soul, seeing perfection,
Natural life of me, faithfully praising things;
Corroborating for ever the triumph of things.

3.

Illustrious every one!
Illustrious what we name space—sphere of unnumbered
    spirits;
Illustrious the mystery of motion, in all beings, even the
    tiniest insect;
Illustrious the attribute of speech—the senses—the body;
Illustrious the passing light! Illustrious the pale reflection
    on the new moon in the western sky!
Illustrious whatever I see, or hear, or touch, to the last.

Good in all,
In the satisfaction and *aplomb* of animals,

In the annual return of the seasons,
In the hilarity of youth,
In the strength and flush of manhood,
In the grandeur and exquisiteness of old age,
In the superb vistas of Death.

Wonderful to depart;
Wonderful to be here!
The heart, to jet the all-alike and innocent blood,
To breathe the air, how delicious!
To speak! to walk! to seize something by the hand!
To prepare for sleep, for bed—to look on my rose-
    coloured flesh,
To be conscious of my body, so happy, so large,
To be this incredible God I am,
To have gone forth among other Gods—those men and
    women I love.

Wonderful how I celebrate you and myself!
How my thoughts play subtly at the spectacles around!
How the clouds pass silently overhead!
How the earth darts on and on! and how the sun, moon,
    stars, dart on and on!
How the water sports and sings! (Surely it is alive!)
How the trees rise and stand up—with strong trunks—
    with branches and leaves!
Surely there is something more in each of the trees—some
    living soul.

O amazement of things! even the least particle!
O spirituality of things!
O strain musical, flowing through ages and continents—
    now reaching me and America!
I take your strong chords—I intersperse them, and
    cheerfully pass them forward.

I too carol the sun, ushered, or at noon, or, as now,
    setting,
I too throb to the brain and beauty of the earth, and of all
    the growths of the earth,
I too have felt the resistless call of myself.

As I sailed down the Mississippi,
As I wandered over the prairies,
As I have lived—As I have looked through my windows,
    my eyes,
As I went forth in the morning—As I beheld the light
    breaking in the east;

As I bathed on the beach of the Eastern Sea, and again on
    the beach of the Western Sea;
As I roamed the streets of inland Chicago-whatever
    streets I have roamed;
Wherever I have been, I have charged myself with
    contentment and triumph.

4.

I sing the Equalities;
I sing the endless finales of things;
I say Nature continues—Glory continues;
I praise with electric voice:
For I do not see one imperfection in the universe;
And I do not see one cause or result lamentable at last in
    the universe.

O setting sun! though the time has come,
I still warble under you unmitigated adoration.

LONGINGS FOR HOME.

O Magnet South! O glistening, perfumed South! my
    South!
O quick mettle, rich blood, impulse, and love! good and
    evil! O all dear to me!
O dear to me my birth-things—all moving things, and
    the trees where I was born,[1] the grains, plants, rivers;
Dear to me my own slow, sluggish rivers, where they flow
    distant over flats of silvery sands or through swamps;
Dear to me the Roanoke, the Savannah, the Altamahaw,
    the Pedee, the Tombigbee, the Santee, the Coosa, and
    the Sabine—
O pensive, far away wandering, I return with my soul to
    haunt their banks again.
Again in Florida I float on transparent lakes—I float on
    Okeechobee—I cross the hummock land, or through
    pleasant openings or dense forests.
I see the parrots in the woods, I see the papaw-tree, and
    the blossoming titi.
Again, sailing in my coaster, on deck, I coast off Georgia,
    I coast up the Carolinas;
I see where the live-oak is growing—I see where the
    yellow-pine, the scented bay-tree, the lemon and
    orange, the cypress, the graceful palmetto.
I pass rude sea-headlands, and enter Pamlico Sound
    through an inlet, and dart my vision inland;
O the cotton plant! the growing fields of rice, sugar, hemp!
The cactus, guarded with thorns—the laurel-tree, with
    large white flowers;

The range afar—the richness and barrenness—the old
  woods charged with mistletoe and trailing moss,
The piney odour and the gloom—the awful natural
  stillness, Here in these dense swamps the freebooter
  carries his gun, and the fugitive slave has his
  concealed hut;
O the strange fascination of these half-known, half-
  impassable swamps, infested by reptiles, resounding
  with the bellow of the alligator, the sad noises of
  the night-owl and the wild-cat, and the whirr of the
  rattlesnake;
The mocking-bird, the American mimic, singing all the
  forenoon—singing through the moon-lit night,
The humming-bird, the wild-turkey, the raccoon, the
  opossum;
A Tennessee corn-field—the tall, graceful, long-leaved
  corn—slender, flapping, bright green, with tassels—
  with beautiful ears, each well-sheathed in its husk;
An Arkansas prairie—a sleeping lake, or still bayou.
O my heart! O tender and fierce pangs—I can stand them
  not—I will depart!
O to be a Virginian, where I grew up! O to be a
  Carolinian!
O longings irrepressible! O I will go back to old
  Tennessee, and never wander more!

FOOTNOTES:

1. *These expressions cannot be understood in a literal sense, for
Whitman was born, not in the South, but in the State of New
York. The precise sense to be attached to them may be open to
some difference of opinion.*

APPEARANCES.

Of the terrible doubt of appearances,
Of the uncertainty after all—that we may be deluded,
That maybe reliance and hope are but speculations after
    all,
That maybe identity beyond the grave is a beautiful fable
    only,
Maybe the things I perceive—the animals, plants, men,
    hills, shining and flowing waters,
The skies of day and night—colours, densities, forms—
    Maybe these are (as doubtless they are) only
    apparitions, and the real something has yet to be
    known;
(How often they dart out of themselves, as if to confound
    me and mock me!
How often I think neither I know, nor any man knows,
    aught of them!)
Maybe seeming to me what they are (as doubtless they
    indeed but seem) as from my present point of view
    —And might prove (as of course they would) naught
    of what they appear, or naught anyhow, from entirely
    changed points of view;
—To me, these, and the like of these, are curiously
    answered by my lovers, my dear friends.
When he whom I love travels with me, or sits a long while
    holding me by the hand,
When the subtle air, the impalpable, the sense that words
    and reason hold not, surround us and pervade us,
Then I am charged with untold and untellable wisdom—I
    am silent—I require nothing further,

I cannot answer the question of appearances, or that of
    identity beyond the grave;
But I walk or sit indifferent—I am satisfied,
He ahold of my hand has completely satisfied me.

THE FRIEND.

Recorders ages hence!
Come, I will take you down underneath this impassive
    exterior—I will tell you what to say of me;
Publish my name and hang up my picture as that of the
    tenderest lover,
The friend, the lover's portrait, of whom his friend, his
    lover, was fondest,
Who was not proud of his songs, but of the measureless
    ocean of love within him—and freely poured it forth,
Who often walked lonesome walks, thinking of his dear
    friends, his lovers,
Who pensive, away from one he loved, often lay sleepless
    and dissatisfied at night,
Who knew too well the sick, sick dread lest the one he
    loved might secretly be indifferent to him,
Whose happiest days were far away, through fields, in
    woods, on hills, he and another, wandering hand in
    hand, they twain, apart from other men,
Who oft, as he sauntered the streets, curved with his
    arm the shoulder of his friend—while the arm of his
    friend rested upon him also.

MEETING AGAIN.

When I heard at the close of the day how my name had
　　been received with plaudits in the capitol, still it was
　　not a happy night for me that followed;
And else, when I caroused, or when my plans were
　　accomplished, still I was not happy.
But the day when I rose at dawn from the bed of perfect
　　health, refreshed, singing, inhaling the ripe breath of
　　autumn,

When I saw the full moon in the west grow pale and
　　disappear in the morning light,
When I wandered alone over the beach, and undressing
　　bathed, laughing with the cool waters, and saw the
　　sunrise,
And when I thought how my dear friend, my lover, was
　　on his way coming, O then I was happy;
O then each breath tasted sweeter—and all that day my
　　food nourished me more—and the beautiful day
　　passed well,

And the next came with equal joy—and with the next, at
　　evening, came my friend;
And that night, while all was still, I heard the waters roll
　　slowly continually up the shores,
I heard the hissing rustle of the liquid and sands, as
　　directed to me, whispering, to congratulate me;
For the one I love most lay sleeping by me under the
　　same cover in the cool night,

In the stillness, in the autumn moonbeams, his face was
    inclined toward me,
And his arm lay lightly around my breast—and that night
    I was happy.

A DREAM.

Of him I love day and night, I dreamed I heard he was
　　dead;
And I dreamed I went where they had buried him I love—
　　but he was not in that place;
And I dreamed I wandered, searching among burial-
　　places, to find him;
And I found that every place was a burial-place;
The houses full of life were equally full of death, (this
　　house is now;)
The streets, the shipping, the places of amusement, the
　　Chicago, Boston,
Philadelphia, the Mannahatta, were as full of the dead as
　　of the living,
And fuller, O vastly fuller, of the dead than of the living.
—And what I dreamed I will henceforth tell to every
　　person and age,
And I stand henceforth bound to what I dreamed;
And now I am willing to disregard burial-places, and
　　dispense with them;
And if the memorials of the dead were put up
　　indifferently everywhere, even in the room where I eat
　　or sleep, I should be satisfied;
And if the corpse of any one I love, or if my own corpse,
　　be duly rendered to powder, and poured in the sea, I
　　shall be satisfied;
Or if it be distributed to the winds, I shall be satisfied.

PARTING FRIENDS.

What think you I take my pen in hand to record?
The battle-ship, perfect-modelled, majestic, that I saw pass
    the offing to- day under full sail?
The splendours of the past day? Or the splendour of the
    night that envelops me?
Or the vaunted glory and growth of the great city spread
    around me?—No;
But I record of two simple men I saw to-day, on the pier,
    in the midst of the crowd, parting the parting of dear
    friends;
The one to remain hung on the other's neck, and
    passionately kissed him,
While the one to depart tightly pressed the one to remain
    in his arms.

TO A STRANGER.

Passing stranger! you do not know how longingly I look
    upon you;
You must be he I was seeking, or she I was seeking (it
    comes to me, as of a dream).
I have somewhere surely lived a life of joy with you.
All is recalled as we flit by each other, fluid, affectionate,
    chaste, matured;
You grew up with me, were a boy with me, or a girl with
    me;
I ate with you, and slept with you—your body has become
    not yours only, nor left my body mine only;
You give me the pleasure of your eyes, face, flesh, as we
    pass—you take of my beard, breast, hands in return;
I am not to speak to you—I am to think of you when I sit
    alone, or wake at night alone;
I am to wait—I do not doubt I am to meet you again;
I am to see to it that I do not lose you.

OTHER LANDS.

This moment yearning and thoughtful, sitting alone,
It seems to me there are other men in other lands,
    yearning and thoughtful;
It seems to me I can look over and behold them in
    Prussia, Italy, France, Spain—or far, far away, in
    China, or in Russia or India—talking other dialects;
And it seems to me, if I could know those men, I should
    become attached to them, as I do to men in my own
    lands.
O I know we should be brethren and lovers;
I know I should be happy with them.

ENVY.

When I peruse the conquered fame of heroes, and
    the victories of mighty generals, I do not envy the
    generals,
Nor the President in his Presidency, nor the rich in his
    great house.
But when I read of the brotherhood of lovers, how it was
    with them;
How through life, through dangers, odium, unchanging,
    long and long,
Through youth, and through middle and old age, how
    unfaltering, how affectionate and faithful they were,
Then I am pensive—I hastily put down the book, and
    walk away, filled with the bitterest envy.

THE CITY OF FRIENDS.

I dreamed in a dream I saw a city invincible to the attacks
    of the whole of the rest of the earth;
I dreamed that it was the new City of Friends;
Nothing was greater there than the quality of robust
    love—it led the rest;
It was seen every hour in the actions of the men of that
    city,
And in all their looks and words.

OUT OF THE CROWD.

1.

Out of the rolling ocean, the crowd, came a drop gently to
    me,
Whispering, *I love you; before long I die:*
I have travelled a long way, merely to look on you, to touch
    you:
For I could not die till I once looked on you,
For I feared I might afterward lose you.

2.

Now we have met, we have looked, we are safe;
Return in peace to the ocean, my love;
I too am part of that ocean, my love—we are not so much
    separated;
Behold the great *rondure*—the cohesion of all, how
    perfect!
But as for me, for you, the irresistible sea is to separate us,
As for an hour carrying us diverse—yet cannot carry us
    diverse for ever;
Be not impatient—a little space—know you, I salute the
    air, the ocean, and the land,
Every day, at sundown, for your dear sake, my love.

AMONG THE MULTITUDE.

Among the men and women, the multitude,
I perceive one picking me out by secret and divine signs,
Acknowledging none else—not parent, wife, husband,
    brother, child, any nearer than I am;
Some are baffled—But that one is not—that one knows
    me.

Ah, lover and perfect equal!
I meant that you should discover me so, by my faint
    indirections;
And I, when I meet you, mean to discover you by the like
    in you.

LEAVES OF GRASS.

PRESIDENT LINCOLN'S FUNERAL HYMN.

1.

When lilacs last in the door-yard bloomed,
And the great star[1] early drooped in the western sky in
    the night,
I mourned,…and yet shall mourn with ever-returning
    spring.

O ever-returning spring! trinity sure to me you bring;
Lilac blooming perennial, and drooping star in the west,
And thought of him I love.

2.

O powerful, western, fallen star!
O shades of night! O moody, tearful night!
O great star disappeared! O the black murk that hides the
    star!
O cruel hands that hold me powerless! O helpless soul of
    me!
O harsh surrounding cloud that will not free my soul!

3.

In the door-yard fronting an old farm-house, near the
    whitewashed palings,
Stands the lilac bush, tall-growing, with heart-shaped
    leaves of rich green,

With many a pointed blossom, rising delicate, with the
    perfume strong I love,
With every leaf a miracle: and from this bush in the
    dooryard,
With delicate-coloured blossoms, and heart-shaped leaves
    of rich green,
A sprig, with its flower, I break.

4.

In the swamp, in secluded recesses,
A shy and hidden bird is warbling a song.

Solitary, the thrush,
The hermit, withdrawn to himself, avoiding the
    settlements,
Sings by himself a song:

Song of the bleeding throat!
Death's outlet song of life—for well, dear brother, I know,
If thou wast not gifted to sing, thou wouldst surely die.

5.

Over the breast of the spring, the land, amid cities,
Amid lanes, and through old woods, where lately
    the violets peeped from the ground, spotting the
    greydebris;
Amid the grass in the fields each side of the lanes—
    passing the endless grass;
Passing the yellow-speared wheat, every grain from its
    shroud in the dark-brown fields uprising;
Passing the apple-tree blows of white and pink in the
    orchards;
Carrying a corpse to where it shall rest in the grave,

Night and day journeys a coffin.

6.

Coffin that passes through lanes and streets,
Through day and night, with the great cloud darkening
the land,
With the pomp of the inlooped flags, with the cities
draped in black,
With the show of the States themselves as of crape-veiled
women standing,
With processions long and winding, and the flambeaus of
the night,
With the countless torches lit—with the silent sea of faces,
and the unbared heads,
With the waiting depot, the arriving coffin, and the
sombre faces,
With dirges through the night, with the thousand voices
rising strong and solemn;
With all the mournful voices of the dirges, poured around
the coffin,
The dim-lit churches and the shuddering organs—Where
amid these you journey,
With the tolling, tolling bells' perpetual clang;
Here! coffin that slowly passes,
I give you my sprig of lilac.

7.

Nor for you, for one, alone;
Blossoms and branches green to coffins all I bring:
For fresh as the morning—thus would I chant a song for
you, O sane and sacred Death.

All over bouquets of roses,

O Death! I cover you over with roses and early lilies;
But mostly and now the lilac that blooms the first,
Copious, I break, I break the sprigs from the bushes!
With loaded arms I come, pouring for you,
For you and the coffins all of you, O Death.

8.

O western orb, sailing the heaven!
Now I know what you must have meant, as a month since
    we walked,
As we walked up and down in the dark blue so mystic,
As we walked in silence the transparent shadowy night,
As I saw you had something to tell, as you bent to me
    night after night,
As you drooped from the sky low down, as if to my side,
    while the other stars all looked on;
As we wandered together the solemn night, for
    something, I know not what, kept me from sleep;
As the night advanced, and I saw on the rim of the west,
    ere you went, how full you were of woe;
As I stood on the rising ground in the breeze, in the cool
    transparent night,
As I watched where you passed and was lost in the
    netherward black of the night,
As my soul, in its trouble, dissatisfied, sank, as where you,
    sad orb,
Concluded, dropped in the night, and was gone.

9.

Sing on, there in the swamp!
O singer bashful and tender! I hear your notes—I hear
    your call;
I hear—I come presently—I understand you;

But a moment I linger—for the lustrous star has detained
    me;
The star, my comrade departing, holds and detains me.

10.

O how shall I warble myself for the dead one there I
    loved?
And how shall I deck my song for the large sweet soul that
    has gone?
And what shall my perfume be for the grave of him I love?

Sea-winds, blown from east and west,
Blown from the Eastern Sea, and blown from the Western
    Sea, till there on the prairies meeting:
These, and with these, and the breath of my chant,
I perfume the grave of him I love.

11.

O what shall I hang on the chamber walls?
And what shall the pictures be that I hang on the walls,
To adorn the burial-house of him I love?

Pictures of growing spring, and farms, and homes,
With the Fourth-month eve at sundown, and the grey
    smoke lucid and bright,
With floods of the yellow gold of the gorgeous, indolent
    sinking sun, burning, expanding the air;
With the fresh sweet herbage under foot, and the pale
    green leaves of the trees prolific;
In the distance the flowing glaze, the breast of the river,
    with a wind-dapple here and there;
With ranging hills on the banks, with many a line against
    the sky, and shadows;

And the city at hand, with dwellings so dense, and stacks
    of chimneys,
And all the scenes of life, and the workshops, and the
    workmen homeward returning.

12.

Lo! body and soul! this land!
Mighty Manhattan, with spires, and the sparkling and
    hurrying tides, and the ships;
The varied and ample land—the South and the North in
    the
light—Ohio's shores, and flashing Missouri,
And ever the far-spreading prairies, covered with grass
    and corn.

Lo! the most excellent sun, so calm and haughty;
The violet and purple morn, with just-felt breezes;
The gentle, soft-born, measureless light;
The miracle, spreading, bathing all—the fulfilled noon;
The coming eve, delicious—the welcome night, and the
    stars,
Over my cities shining all, enveloping man and land.

13.

Sing on! sing on, you grey-brown bird!
Sing from the swamps, the recesses—pour your chant
    from the bushes;
Limitless out of the dusk, out of the cedars and pines.

Sing on, dearest brother—warble your reedy song,
Loud human song, with voice of uttermost woe.

O liquid, and free, and tender!

O wild and loose to my soul! O wondrous singer!
You only I hear,… yet the star holds me, (but will soon
    depart;)
Yet the lilac, with mastering odour, holds me.

14.

Now while I sat in the day, and looked forth,
In the close of the day, with its light, and the fields of
    spring, and the farmer preparing his crops,
In the large unconscious scenery of my land, with its lakes
    and forests,
In the heavenly aerial beauty, after the perturbed winds
    and the storms;
Under the arching heavens of the afternoon swift passing,
    and the voices of children and women,
The many-moving sea-tides,—and I saw the ships how
    they sailed,
And the summer approaching with richness, and the
    fields all busy with labour,
And the infinite separate houses, how they all went on,
    each with its meals
and minutiae of daily usages;
And the streets, how their throbbings throbbed, and the
    cities pent—lo! then and there,
Falling upon them all, and among them all, enveloping
    me with the rest,
Appeared the cloud, appeared the long black trail;
And I knew Death, its thought, and the sacred knowledge
    of Death.

15.

And the Thought of Death close-walking the other side of
    me,

And I in the middle, as with companions, and as holding
    the hands of companions,
I fled forth to the hiding receiving night, that talks not,
Down to the shores of the water, the path by the swamp in
    the dimness,
To the solemn shadowy cedars, and ghostly pines so still.

And the singer so shy to the rest received me;
The grey-brown bird I know received us Comrades three;
And he sang what seemed the song of Death, and a verse
    for him I love.

From deep secluded recesses,
From the fragrant cedars, and the ghostly pines so still,
Came the singing of the bird.

And the charm of the singing rapt me,
As I held, as if by their hands, my Comrades in the night;
And the voice of my spirit tallied the song of the bird.

16.

Come, lovely and soothing Death,
Undulate round the world, serenely arriving, arriving,
In the day, in the night, to all, to each,
Sooner or later, delicate Death.

Praised be the fathomless universe,
For life and joy, and for objects and knowledge curious;
And for love, sweet love—But praise! O praise and praise,
For the sure-enwinding arms of cool-enfolding Death.

Dark Mother, always gliding near, with soft feet,
Have none chanted for thee a chant of fullest welcome?
Then I chant it for thee—I glorify thee above all;

I bring thee a song that, when thou must indeed come,
    come unfalteringly.

Approach, encompassing Death-strong deliveress!
When it is so—when thou hast taken them, I joyously sing
    the dead,
Lost in the loving, floating ocean of thee,
Laved in the flood of thy bliss, O Death.

From me to thee glad serenades,
Dances for thee I propose, saluting thee—adornments
    and feastings for thee;
And the sights of the open landscape, and the high-spread
    sky, are fitting,
And life and the fields, and the huge and thoughtful
    night.

The night, in silence, under many a star;
The ocean shore, and the husky whispering wave, whose
    voice I know;
And the soul turning to thee, O vast and well-veiled
    Death,
And the body gratefully nestling close to thee.

Over the tree-tops I float thee a song!
Over the rising and sinking waves—over the myriad
    fields, and the prairies wide;
Over the dense-packed cities all, and the teeming wharves
    and ways,
I float this carol with joy, with joy, to thee, O Death!

17.

To the tally of my soul
Loud and strong kept up the grey-brown bird,

With pure, deliberate notes, spreading, filling the night.

Loud in the pines and cedars dim,
Clear in the freshness moist, and the swamp-perfume,
And I with my Comrades there in the night.

While my sight that was bound in my eyes unclosed,
As to long panoramas of visions.

18.

I saw the vision of armies;
And I saw, as in noiseless dreams, hundreds of battle-
flags;
Borne through the smoke of the battles, and pierced with
missiles, I saw them,
And carried hither and yon through the smoke, and torn
and bloody;
And at last but a few shreds of the flags left on the staffs,
(and all in silence,)
And the staffs all splintered and broken.

I saw battle-corpses, myriads of them,
And the white skeletons of young men—I saw them;
I saw the debris and debris of all dead soldiers.
But I saw they were not as was thought;
They themselves were fully at rest—they suffered not;
The living remained and suffered—the mother suffered,
And the wife and the child, and the musing comrade
suffered,
And the armies that remained suffered.

19.

Passing the visions, passing the night;

Passing, unloosing the hold of my Comrades' hands;
Passing the song of the hermit bird, and the tallying song
    of my soul;
Victorious song, Death's outlet song, yet varying, ever-
    altering song;
As low and wailing, yet clear, the notes, rising and falling,
    flooding the night,
Sadly sinking and fainting, as warning and warning, and
    yet again bursting with joy.
Covering the earth, and filling the spread of the heaven,
As that powerful psalm in the night, I heard from
    recesses.

20.

Must I leave thee, lilac with heart-shaped leaves?
Must I leave thee there in the door-yard, blooming,
    returning with spring?

Must I pass from my song for thee—
From my gaze on thee in the west, fronting the west,
    communing with thee,
O comrade lustrous, with silver face in the night?

21.

Yet each I keep, and all;
The song, the wondrous chant of the grey-brown bird,
And the tallying chant, the echo aroused in my soul,
With the lustrous and drooping star, with the
    countenance full of woe;
With the lilac tali, and its blossoms of mastering odour;
Comrades mine, and I in the midst, and their memory
    ever I keep—for the dead I loved so well;

For the sweetest, wisest soul of all my days and lands—
    and this for his dear sake;
Lilac and star and bird, twined with the chant of my soul,
With the holders holding my hand, nearing the call of the
    bird,
There in the fragrant pines, and the cedars dusk and dim.

FOOTNOTES :

1. *"The evening star, which, as many may remember night
after night, in the early part of that eventful spring, hung
low in the west with unusual and tender brightness."—
JOHN BURROUGHS.*

O CAPTAIN! MY CAPTAIN!

(For the death of Lincoln.)

1.

O Captain! my Captain! our fearful trip is done!
The ship has weathered every wrack, the prize we sought
    is won.
The port is near, the bells I hear, the people all exulting,
While follow eyes the steady keel, the vessel grim and
    daring.
        But, O heart! heart! heart!
        Leave you not the little spot
        Where on the deck my Captain lies,
            Fallen cold and dead.

2.

O Captain! my Captain! rise up and hear the bells!
Rise up! for you the flag is flung, for you the bugle trills:
For you bouquets and ribboned wreaths; for you the
    shores a-crowding:
For you they call, the swaying mass, their eager faces
    turning.
        O Captain! dear father!
        This arm I push beneath you.
        It is some dream that on the deck
            You've fallen cold and dead!

3.

My Captain does not answer, his lips are pale and still:
My father does not feel my arm, he has no pulse nor will.
But the ship, the ship is anchored safe, its voyage closed
    and done:
From fearful trip the victor ship comes in with object
    won!
              Exult, O shores! and ring, O bells!
              But I, with silent tread,
              Walk the spot my Captain lies,
                  Fallen cold and dead.

PIONEERS! O PIONEERS!

_____

1.

Come, my tan-faced children,
Follow well in order, get your weapons ready;
Have you your pistols? have you your sharp-edged axes?
    Pioneers! O pioneers!

2.

For we cannot tarry here,
We must march, my darlings, we must bear the brunt of
    danger,
We, the youthful sinewy races, all the rest on us depend.
    Pioneers! O pioneers!

3.

O you youths, Western youths,
So impatient, full of action, full of manly pride and
    friendship,
Plain I see you, Western youths, see you tramping with
    the foremost,
    Pioneers! O pioneers!

4.

Have the elder races halted?
Do they droop and end their lesson, wearied, over there
    beyond the seas?

We take up the task eternal, and the burden, and the
    lesson,
        Pioneers! O pioneers!

5.

All the past we leave behind;
We debouch upon a newer, mightier world, varied world;
Fresh and strong the world we seize, world of labour and
    the march,
        Pioneers! O pioneers!

6.

We detachments steady throwing,
Down the edges, through the passes, up the mountains
    steep,
Conquering, holding, daring, venturing, as we go, the
    unknown ways,
        Pioneers! O pioneers!

7.

We primeval forests felling,
We the rivers stemming, vexing we, and piercing deep the
    mines within;
We the surface broad surveying, and the virgin soil
    upheaving,
        Pioneers! O pioneers!

8.

Colorado men are we,
From the peaks gigantic, from the great sierras and the
    high plateaus,

From the mine and from the gully, from the hunting trail
    we come,
        Pioneers! O pioneers!

9.

    From Nebraska, from Arkansas,
Central inland race are we, from Missouri, with the
    continental blood
interveined;
All the hands of comrades clasping, all the Southern, all
    the Northern,
        Pioneers! O pioneers!

10.

    O resistless, restless race!
O beloved race in all! O my breast aches with tender love
    for all!
O I mourn and yet exult—I am rapt with love for all,
        Pioneers! O pioneers;

11.

    Raise the mighty mother mistress,
Waving high the delicate mistress, over all the starry
    mistress, (bend your
heads all,)
Raise the fanged and warlike mistress, stern, impassive,
    weaponed mistress,
        Pioneers! O pioneers!

12.

See, my children, resolute children,

291

By those swarms upon our rear, we must never yield or
falter,
Ages back in ghostly millions, frowning there behind us
urging,
   Pioneers! O pioneers!

13.

On and on, the compact ranks,
With accessions ever waiting, with the places of the dead
quickly filled,
Through the battle, through defeat, moving yet and never
stopping,
   Pioneers! O pioneers!

14.

O to die advancing on!
Are there some of us to droop and die? has the hour
come?
Then upon the march we fittest die, soon and sure the gap
is filled,
   Pioneers! O pioneers!

15.

All the pulses of the world,
Falling in, they beat for us, with the Western movement
beat;
Holding single or together, steady moving, to the front, all
for us,
   Pioneers! O pioneers!

16.

Life's involved and varied pageants,
All the forms and shows, all the workmen at their work,
All the seamen and the landsmen, all the masters with
    their slaves,
        Pioneers, O pioneers!

17.

All the hapless silent lovers,
All the prisoners in the prisons, all the righteous and the
    wicked,
All the joyous, all the sorrowing, all the living, all the
    dying,
        Pioneers! O pioneers!

18.

I too with my soul and body,
We, a curious trio, picking, wandering on our way,
Through these shores, amid the shadows, with the
    apparitions pressing,
        Pioneers! O pioneers!

19.

Lo! the darting, bowling orb!
Lo! the brother orbs around! all the clustering suns and
    planets;
All the dazzling days, all the mystic nights with dreams,
        Pioneers! O pioneers!

20.

These are of us, they are with us,
All for primal needed work, while the followers there in
    embryo wait
behind,
We to-day's procession heading, we the route for travel
    clearing,
        Pioneers! O pioneers!

21.

O you daughters of the West!
O you young and elder daughters! O you mothers and you
    wives!
Never must you be divided, in our ranks you move
    united,
        Pioneers! O pioneers!

22.

Minstrels latent on the prairies!
(Shrouded bards of other lands! you may sleep—you have
    done your work;)
Soon I hear you coming warbling, soon you rise and
    tramp amid us,
        Pioneers! O pioneers!

23.

Not for delectations sweet;
Not the cushion and the slipper, not the peaceful and the
    studious;
Not the riches safe and palling, not for us the tame
    enjoyment,

Pioneers! O pioneers!

24.

Do the feasters gluttonous feast?
Do the corpulent sleepers sleep? have they locked and
  bolted doors?
Still be ours the diet hard, and the blanket on the ground,
          Pioneers! O pioneers!

25.

Has the night descended?
Was the road of late so toilsome? did we stop discouraged,
  nodding on our
way?
Yet a passing hour I yield you in your tracks to pause
  oblivious,
          Pioneers! O pioneers!

26.

Till with sound of trumpet,
Far, far off the daybreak call—hark! how loud and clear I
  hear it wind;
Swift! to the head of the army!—swift! spring to your
  places,
          Pioneers! O pioneers!

TO THE SAYERS OF WORDS.

1.

Earth, round, rolling, compact—suns, moons, animals—
    all these are words to be said;
Watery, vegetable, sauroid advances—beings,
    premonitions, lispings of the future,
Behold! these are vast words to be said.

Were you thinking that those were the words—those
    upright lines? those curves, angles, dots?
No, those are not the words—the substantial words are in
    the ground and sea,
They are in the air—they are in you.

Were you thinking that those were the words—those
    delicious sounds out of your friends' mouths? No; the
    real words are more delicious than they.

Human bodies are words, myriads of words;
In the best poems reappears the body, man's or woman's,
    well-shaped, natural, gay;
Every part able, active, receptive, without shame or the
    need of shame.

Air, soil, water, fire—these are words;
I myself am a word with them—my qualities
    interpenetrate with theirs—my name is nothing to
    them;

Though it were told in the three thousand languages, what
would air, soil, water, fire, know of my name?

A healthy presence, a friendly or commanding gesture,
are words, sayings, meanings;
The charms that go with the mere looks of some men and
women are sayings and meanings also.

2.

The workmanship of souls is by the inaudible words of the
earth;
The great masters know the earth's words, and use them
more than the audible words.

Amelioration is one of the earth's words;
The earth neither lags nor hastens;
It has all attributes, growths, effects, latent in itself from
the jump;
It is not half beautiful only—defects and excrescences
show just as much as perfections show.

The earth does not withhold—it is generous enough;
The truths of the earth continually wait, they are not so
concealed either;
They are calm, subtle, untransmissible by print;
They are imbued through all things, conveying
themselves willingly,
Conveying a sentiment and invitation of the earth. I utter
and utter:
I speak not; yet, if you hear me not, of what avail am I to
you?
To bear—to better; lacking these, of what avail am I?

Accouche! Accouchez!

Will you rot your own fruit in yourself there?
Will you squat and stifle there?

The earth does not argue,
Is not pathetic, has no arrangements,
Does not scream, haste, persuade, threaten, promise,
Makes no discriminations, has no conceivable failures,
Closes nothing, refuses nothing, shuts none out;
Of all the powers, objects, states, it notifies, shuts none
    out.

The earth does not exhibit itself, nor refuse to exhibit
    itself—possesses still underneath;
Underneath the ostensible sounds, the august chorus of
    heroes, the wail of slaves,
Persuasions of lovers, curses, gasps of the dying, laughter
    of young people, accents of bargainers,
Underneath these, possessing the words that never fail.

To her children, the words of the eloquent dumb great
    Mother never fail;
The true words do not fail, for motion does not fail, and
    reflection does not fail;
Also the day and night do not fail, and the voyage we
    pursue does not fail.

3.

Of the interminable sisters,
Of the ceaseless cotillons of sisters,
Of the centripetal and centrifugal sisters, the elder and
    younger sisters,
The beautiful sister we know dances on with the rest.

With her ample back towards every beholder,

With the fascinations of youth, and the equal fascinations
    of age,
Sits she whom I too love like the rest—sits undisturbed,
Holding up in her hand what has the character of a
    mirror, while her eyes glance back from it,
Glance as she sits, inviting none, denying none,
Holding a mirror day and night tirelessly before her own
    face.

Seen at hand, or seen at a distance,
Duly the twenty-four appear in public every day,
Duly approach and pass with their companions, or a
    companion,
Looking from no countenances of their own, but from the
    countenances of those who are with them,
From the countenances of children or women, or the
    manly countenance,
From the open countenances of animals, or from
    inanimate things,
From the landscape or waters, or from the exquisite
    apparition of the sky,
From our countenances, mine and yours, faithfully
    returning them,
Every day in public appearing without fail, but never
    twice with the same companions.

Embracing man, embracing all, proceed the three
    hundred and sixty-five resistlessly round the sun;
Embracing all, soothing, supporting, follow close three
    hundred and sixty- five offsets of the first, sure and
    necessary as they.

Tumbling on steadily, nothing dreading,
Sunshine, storm, cold, heat, for ever withstanding,
    passing, carrying,

The Soul's realisation and determination still inheriting;
The fluid vacuum around and ahead still entering and
    dividing,
No baulk retarding, no anchor anchoring, on no rock
    striking,
Swift, glad, content, unbereaved, nothing losing,
Of all able and ready at any time to give strict account,
The divine ship sails the divine sea.

4.

Whoever you are! motion and reflection are especially for
    you;
The divine ship sails the divine sea for you.

Whoever you are! you are he or she for whom the earth is
    solid and liquid,
You are he or she for whom the sun and moon hang in the
    sky;
For none more than you are the present and the past,
For none more than you is immortality.

Each man to himself, and each woman to herself, such
    as the word of the past and present, and the word of
    immortality;
No one can acquire for another—not one!
Not one can grow for another—not one!

The song is to the singer, and comes back most to him;
The teaching is to the teacher, and comes back most to
    him;
The murder is to the murderer, and comes back most to
    him;
The theft is to the thief, and comes back most to him;
The love is to the lover, and conies back most to him;

The gift is to the giver, and comes back most to him—it
    cannot fail;
The oration is to the orator, the acting is to the actor and
    actress, not to the audience;
And no man understands any greatness or goodness but
    his own, or the indication of his own.

5.

I swear the earth shall surely be complete to him or her
    who shall be complete!
I swear the earth remains jagged and broken only to him
    or her who remains broken and jagged!

I swear there is no greatness or power that does not
    emulate those of the earth!
I swear there can be no theory of any account, unless it
    corroborate the theory of the earth!

No politics, art, religion, behaviour, or what not, is of
    account, unless it compare with the amplitude of the
    earth,
Unless it face the exactness, vitality, impartiality,
    rectitude, of the earth.

I swear I begin to see love with sweeter spasms than that
    which responds love!
It is that which contains itself—which never invites, and
    never refuses.

I swear I begin to see little or nothing in audible words!
I swear I think all merges toward the presentation of the
    unspoken meanings of the earth;
Toward him who sings the songs of the Body, and of the
    truths of the earth;

Toward him who makes the dictionaries of words that
  print cannot touch.

I swear I see what is better than to tell the best;
It is always to leave the best untold.

When I undertake to tell the best, I find I cannot,
My tongue is ineffectual on its pivots,
My breath will not be obedient to its organs,
I become a dumb man.

The best of the earth cannot be told anyhow—all or any is
  best;
It is not what you anticipated—it is cheaper, easier, nearer;
Things are not dismissed from the places they held before;
The earth is just as positive and direct as it was before;
Facts, religions, improvements, politics, trades, are as real
  as before;
But the Soul is also real,—it too is positive and direct;
No reasoning, no proof has established it,
Undeniable growth has established it.

6.

This is a poem for the sayers of words—these are hints of
  meanings,
These are they that echo the tones of souls, and the
  phrases of souls;
If they did not echo the phrases of souls, what were they
  then?
If they had not reference to you in especial, what were
  they then?

I swear I will never henceforth have to do with the faith
  that tells the best!

I will have to do only with that faith that leaves the best
untold.

7.

Say on, sayers!
Delve! mould! pile the words of the earth!
Work on—it is materials you bring, not breaths;
Work on, age after age! nothing is to be lost!
It may have to wait long, but it will certainly come in use;
When the materials are all prepared, the architects shall
appear.

I swear to you the architects shall appear without fail! I
announce them and lead them;
I swear to you they will understand you and justify you;
I swear to you the greatest among them shall be he who
best knows you, and encloses all, and is faithful to all;
I swear to you, he and the rest shall not forget you—they
shall perceive that you are not an iota less than they;
I swear to you, you shall be glorified in them.

VOICES.

1.

Now I make a leaf of Voices—for I have found nothing
  mightier than they are,
And I have found that no word spoken but is beautiful in
  its place.

2.

O what is it in me that makes me tremble so at voices?
Surely, whoever speaks to me in the right voice, him or
  her I shall follow,
As the water follows the moon, silently, with fluid steps
  anywhere around the globe.

All waits for the right voices;
Where is the practised and perfect organ? Where is the
  developed Soul?
For I see every word uttered thence has deeper, sweeter,
  new sounds, impossible on less terms.

I see brains and lips closed—tympans and temples
  unstruck,
Until that comes which has the quality to strike and to
  unclose,
Until that comes which has the quality to bring forth
  what lies slumbering, for ever ready, in all words.

WHOSOEVER.

Whoever you are, I fear you are walking the walks of
dreams,
I fear those supposed realities are to melt from under your
feet and hands;
Even now, your features, joys, speech, house, trade,
manners, troubles, follies, costume, crimes, dissipate
away from you,
Your true Soul and Body appear before me,
They stand forth out of affairs-out of commerce,
shops, law, science, work, farms, clothes, the house,
medicine, print, buying, selling, eating, drinking,
suffering, dying.

Whoever you are, now I place my hand upon you, that
you be my poem;
I whisper with my lips close to your ear,
I have loved many women and men, but I love none better
than you.
Oh! I have been dilatory and dumb;
I should have made my way straight to you long ago;
I should have blabbed nothing but you, I should have
chanted nothing but you.

I will leave all, and come and make the hymns of you;
None have understood you, but I understand you;
None have done justice to you—you have not done justice
to yourself;
None but have found you imperfect—I only find no
imperfection in you;

None but would subordinate you—I only am he who will
    never consent to subordinate you;
I only am he who places over you no master, owner, better,
    God, beyond what waits intrinsically in yourself.

Painters have painted their swarming groups, and the
    centre figure of all,
From the head of the centre figure spreading a nimbus of
    gold-coloured light;
But I paint myriads of heads, but paint no head without
    its nimbus of gold- coloured light;
From my hand, from the brain of every man and woman,
    it streams, effulgently flowing for ever.

O I could sing such grandeurs and glories about you!
You have not known what you are—you have slumbered
    upon yourself all your life;
Your eyelids have been the same as closed most of the
    time;
What you have done returns already in mockeries;
Your thrift, knowledge, prayers, if they do not return in
    mockeries, what is their return?

The mockeries are not you;
Underneath them, and within them, I see you lurk;
I pursue you where none else has pursued you;
Silence, the desk, the flippant expression, the night, the
    accustomed routine, if these conceal you from others,
    or from yourself, they do not conceal you from me;
The shaved face, the unsteady eye, the impure
    complexion, if these baulk others, they do not baulk
    me.
The pert apparel, the deformed attitude, drunkenness,
    greed, premature death, all these I part aside.

There is no endowment in man or woman that is not
  tallied in you;
There is no virtue, no beauty, in man or woman, but as
  good is in you;
No pluck, no endurance in others, but as good is in you;
No pleasure waiting for others, but an equal pleasure
  waits for you.
As for me, I give nothing to any one, except I give the like
  carefully to you;
I sing the songs of the glory of none, not God, sooner than
  I sing the songs of the glory of you.

Whoever you are! claim your own at any hazard!
These shows of the east and west are tame compared to
  you;
These immense meadows—these interminable rivers—
  you are immense and interminable as they;
These furies, elements, storms, motions of Nature, throes
  of apparent dissolution—you are he or she who is
  master or mistress over them,
Master or mistress in your own right over Nature,
  elements, pain, passion, dissolution.

The hopples fall from your ankles—you find an unfailing
  sufficiency;
Old or young, male or female, rude, low, rejected by the
  rest, whatever you are promulgates itself; T
hrough birth, life, death, burial, the means are provided,
  nothing is scanted;
Through angers, losses, ambition, ignorance, ennui, what
  you are picks its way.

BEGINNERS.

How they are provided for upon the earth, appearing at
    intervals;
How dear and dreadful they are to the earth;
How they inure to themselves as much as to any—What a
    paradox appears their age;
How people respond to them, yet know them not;
How there is something relentless in their fate, all times;
How all times mischoose the objects of their adulation
    and reward,
And how the same inexorable price must still be paid for
    the same great purchase.

TO A PUPIL.

1.

Is reform needed? Is it through you?
The greater the reform needed, the greater the
  PERSONALITY you need to accomplish it.

You! do you not see how it would serve to have eyes,
  blood, complexion, clean and sweet?

Do you not see how it would serve to have such a
  Body and Soul that, when you enter the crowd, an
  atmosphere of desire and command enters with you,
  and every one is impressed with your personality?

2.

O the magnet! the flesh over and over!
Go, dear friend! if need be, give up all else, and
  commence to-day to inure yourself to pluck, reality,
  self-esteem, definiteness, elevatedness;
Rest not, till you rivet and publish yourself of your own
  personality.

LINKS.

1.

Think of the Soul;
I swear to you that body of yours gives proportions to
    your Soul somehow to live in other spheres;
I do not know how, but I know it is so.

2.

Think of loving and being loved;
I swear to you, whoever you are, you can interfuse
    yourself with such things that everybody that sees you
    shall look longingly upon you.

3.

Think of the past;
I warn you that, in a little while, others will find their past
    in you and your times.

The race is never separated—nor man nor woman
    escapes; All is inextricable—things, spirits, nature,
    nations, you too—from precedents you come.

Recall the ever-welcome defiers (the mothers precede
    them);
Recall the sages, poets, saviours, inventors, lawgivers, of
    the earth;

Recall Christ, brother of rejected persons—brother of
   slaves, felons, idiots, and of insane and diseased
   persons.

4.

Think of the time when you was not yet born;
Think of times you stood at the side of the dying;
Think of the time when your own body will be dying.

Think of spiritual results:
Sure as the earth swims through the heavens, does every
   one of its objects pass into spiritual results.

Think of manhood, and you to be a man;
Do you count manhood, and the sweet of manhood,
   nothing?

Think of womanhood, and you to be a woman;
The creation is womanhood;
Have I not said that womanhood involves all?
Have I not told how the universe has nothing better than
   the best womanhood?

THE WATERS.

The world below the brine.
Forests at the bottom of the sea—the branches and leaves,
Sea-lettuce, vast lichens, strange flowers and seeds—the
thick tangle, the openings, and the pink turf,
Different colours, pale grey and green, purple, white, and
gold—the play of light through the water,
Dumb swimmers there among the rocks—coral, gluten,
grass, rushes—and the aliment of the swimmers,
Sluggish existences grazing there, suspended, or slowly
crawling close to the bottom:
The sperm-whale at the surface, blowing air and spray, or
disporting with his flukes,
The leaden-eyed shark, the walrus, the turtle, the hairy
sea-leopard, and the sting-ray.
Passions there, wars, pursuits, tribes—sight in those
ocean-depths— breathing that thick breathing air, as
so many do.
The change thence to the sight here, and to the subtle air
breathed by beings like us, who walk this sphere:
The change onward from ours to that of beings who walk
other spheres.

TO THE STATES.

To identify the 16th, 17th, or 18th presidentiad.[1]

Why reclining, interrogating? Why myself and all
    drowsing?
What deepening twilight! Scum floating atop of the
    waters!
Who are they, as bats and night-dogs, askant in the
    Capitol?
What a filthy Presidentiad! (O South, your torrid suns! O
    North, your Arctic freezings!)
Are those really Congressmen? Are those the great
    Judges? Is that the President?
Then I will sleep a while yet—for I see that these States
    sleep, for reasons.
With gathering murk—with muttering thunder and
    lambent shoots, we all duly awake,
South, North, East, West, inland and seaboard, we will
    surely awake.

FOOTNOTES :

1. *These were the three Presidentships of Polk; of Taylor, succeeded
    by Fillmore; and of Pierce;—1845 to 1857.*

TEARS.

Tears! tears! tears!
In the night, in solitude, tears;
On the white shore dripping, dripping, sucked in by the
     sand;
Tears—not a star shining—all dark and desolate;
Moist tears from the eyes of a muffled head:
—O who is that ghost?—that form in the dark, with tears?
What shapeless lump is that, bent, crouched there on the
     sand?
Streaming tears—sobbing tears—throes, choked with
     wild cries;
O storm, embodied, rising, careering, with swift steps
     along the beach;
O wild and dismal night-storm, with wind! O belching
     and desperate!
O shade, so sedate and decorous by day, with calm
     countenance and regulated pace;
But away, at night, as you fly, none looking—O then the
     unloosened ocean
Of tears! tears! tears!

A SHIP.

1.

Aboard, at the ship's helm,
A young steersman, steering with care.

A bell through fog on a sea-coast dolefully ringing,
An ocean-bell—O a warning bell, rocked by the waves.

O you give good notice indeed, you bell by the sea-reefs
    ringing,
Ringing, ringing, to warn the ship from its wreck-place.

For, as on the alert, O steersman, you mind the bell's
    admonition,
The bows turn,—the freighted ship, tacking, speeds away
    under her grey sails;
The beautiful and noble ship, with all her precious wealth,
    speeds away gaily and safe.

2.

But O the ship, the immortal ship! O ship aboard the
    ship!
O ship of the body—ship of the soul—voyaging, voyaging,
    voyaging.

GREATNESS.

***

1.

Great are the myths—I too delight in them;
Great are Adam and Eve—I too look back and accept
    them;
Great the risen and fallen nations, and their poets,
    women, sages, inventors, rulers, warriors, and priests.
Great is Liberty! great is Equality! I am their follower;
Helmsmen of nations, choose your craft! where you sail,
    I sail,
I weather it out with you, or sink with you.
Great is Youth—equally great is Old Age—great are the
    Day and Night;
Great is Wealth—great is Poverty—great is Expression—
    great is Silence.

2.

Youth, large, lusty, loving—Youth, full of grace, force,
    fascination!
Do you know that Old Age may come after you, with
    equal grace, force, fascination?

Day, full-blown and splendid—Day of the immense sun,
    action, ambition, laughter,
The Night follows close, with millions of suns, and sleep,
    and restoring darkness.

Wealth, with the flush hand, fine clothes, hospitality;

But then the soul's wealth, which is candour, knowledge,
    pride, enfolding love;
Who goes for men and women showing Poverty richer
    than wealth?

Expression of speech! in what is written or said, forget not
    that Silence is also expressive;
That anguish as hot as the hottest, and contempt as cold
    as the coldest, may be without words.

3.

Great is the Earth, and the way it became what it is:
Do you imagine it has stopped at this? the increase
    abandoned?
Understand then that it goes as far onward from this as
    this is from the times when it lay in covering waters
    and gases, before man had appeared.

4.

Great is the quality of Truth in man;
The quality of truth in man supports itself through all
    changes;
It is inevitably in the man—he and it are in love, and
    never leave each other.

The truth in man is no dictum, it is vital as eyesight;
If there be any Soul, there is truth—if there be man or
    woman, there is truth—if there be physical or moral,
    there is truth;
If there be equilibrium or volition, there is truth—if there
    be things at all upon the earth, there is truth.

O truth of the earth! O truth of things! I am determined
    to press my way toward you;
Sound your voice! I scale mountains, or dive in the sea,
    after you.

5.

Great is Language—it is the mightiest of the sciences,
It is the fulness, colour, form, diversity of the earth, and of
    men and women, and of all qualities and processes;
It is greater than wealth, it is greater than buildings, ships,
    religions, paintings, music.

Great is the English speech—what speech is so great as
    the English?
Great is the English brood—what brood has so vast a
    destiny as the English?
It is the mother of the brood that must rule the earth with
    the new rule;
The new rule shall rule as the Soul rules, and as the love,
    justice, equality in the Soul rule.

6.

Great is Law—great are the old few landmarks of the law,
They are the same in all times, and shall not be disturbed.

Great is Justice!
Justice is not settled by legislators and laws—it is in the
    Soul;
It cannot be varied by statutes, any more than love, pride,
    the attraction of gravity, can;

It is immutable—it does not depend on majorities—
    majorities or what not come at last before the same
    passionless and exact tribunal.

For justice are the grand natural lawyers, and perfect
    judges—it is in their souls;
It is well assorted—they have not studied for nothing—
    the great includes the less;
They rule on the highest grounds—they oversee all eras,
    states, administrations.

The perfect judge fears nothing—he could go front to
    front before God;
Before the perfect judge all shall stand back—life and
    death shall stand back—heaven and hell shall stand
    back.

7.

Great is Life, real and mystical, wherever and whoever;
Great is Death—sure as Life holds all parts together,
    Death holds all parts together.

Has Life much purport?—Ah! Death has the greatest
    purport.

THE POET.

1.

Now list to my morning's romanza;
To the cities and farms I sing, as they spread in the
    sunshine before me.

2.

A young man came to me bearing a message from his
    brother;
How should the young man know the whether and when
    of his brother?
Tell him to send me the signs.

And I stood before the young man face to face, and took
    his right hand in my left hand, and his left hand in my
    right hand,
And I answered for his brother, and for men, and I
    answered for THE POET, and sent these signs.

Him all wait for—him all yield up to—his word is decisive
    and final,
Him they accept, in him lave, in him perceive themselves,
    as amid light,
Him they immerse, and he immerses them.
Beautiful women, the haughtiest nations, laws, the
    landscape, people, animals,
The profound earth and its attributes, and the unquiet
    ocean (so tell I my morning's romanza),

All enjoyments and properties, and money, and whatever
    money will buy,
The best farms—others toiling and planting, and he
    unavoidably reaps,
The noblest and costliest cities—others grading and
    building, and he domiciles there,
Nothing for any one but what is for him—near and far are
    for him,—the ships in the offing,
The perpetual shows and marches on land, are for him, if
    they are for anybody.

He puts things in their attitudes;
He puts to-day out of himself, with plasticity and love;
He places his own city, times, reminiscences, parents,
    brothers and sisters, associations, employment,
    politics, so that the rest never shame them afterward,
    nor assume to command them.

He is the answerer;
What can be answered he answers—and what cannot be
    answered, he shows how it cannot be answered.

3.

A man is a summons and challenge;
(It is vain to skulk—Do you hear that mocking and
    laughter? Do you hear the ironical echoes?)

Books, friendships, philosophers, priests, action, pleasure,
    pride, beat up and down, seeking to give satisfaction;
He indicates the satisfaction, and indicates them that beat
    up and down also.

Whichever the sex, whatever the season or place, he may
    go freshly and gently and safely, by day or by night;

He has the pass-key of hearts—to him the response of the
prying of hands on the knobs.

His welcome is universal—the flow of beauty is not more
welcome or universal than he is;
The person he favours by day or sleeps with at night is
blessed.

Every existence has its idiom—everything has an idiom
and tongue;
He resolves all tongues into his own, and bestows it upon
men, and any man translates, and any man translates
himself also;
One part does not counteract another part—he is the
joiner—he sees how they join.
He says indifferently and alike, "*How are you, friend*?" to
the President at his levee,
And he says, "*Good-day, my brother!*" to Cudge that hoes
in the sugar- field,
And both understand him, and know that his speech is
right.

He walks with perfect ease in the Capitol,
He walks among the Congress, and one representative
says to another, "*Here is our equal, appearing and
new.*"

4.

Then the mechanics take him for a mechanic,
And the soldiers suppose him to be a soldier, and the
sailors that he has followed the sea,
And the authors take him for an author, and the artists
for an artist,

And the labourers perceive he could labour with them
    and love them;
No matter what the work is, that he is the one to follow it,
    or has followed it,
No matter what the nation, that he might find his brothers
    and sisters there.

The English believe he comes of their English stock,
A Jew to the Jew he seems—a Russ to the Russ—usual and
    near, removed from none.

Whoever he looks at in the travellers' coffee-house claims
    him;
The Italian or Frenchman is sure, and the German is sure,
    and the Spaniard is sure, and the island Cuban is sure;
The engineer, the deck-hand on the great lakes, or on
    the Mississippi, or St. Lawrence, or Sacramento, or
    Hudson, or Paumanok Sound, claims him.

The gentleman of perfect blood acknowledges his perfect
    blood;
The insulter, the prostitute, the angry person, the beggar,
    see themselves in the ways of him—he strangely
    transmutes them,
They are not vile any more—they hardly know
    themselves, they are so grown.

BURIAL.

1.

To think of it!
To think of time—of all that retrospection!
To think of to-day, and the ages continued henceforward!
Have you guessed you yourself would not continue?
Have you dreaded these earth-beetles?
Have you feared the future would be nothing to you?
Is to-day nothing? Is the beginningless past nothing?
If the future is nothing, they are just as surely nothing.

To think that the sun rose in the east! that men and
    women were flexible, real, alive! that everything was
    alive!
To think that you and I did not see, feel, think, nor bear
    our part!
To think that we are now here, and bear our part!

2.

Not a day passes—not a minute or second, without an
    accouchement!
Not a day passes-not a minute or second, without a
    corpse!

The dull nights go over, and the dull days also,
The soreness of lying so much in bed goes over,
The physician, after long putting off, gives the silent and
    terrible look for an answer,

The children come hurried and weeping, and the brothers
    and sisters are sent for;
Medicines stand unused on the shelf—(the camphor-
    smell has long pervaded the rooms,)
The faithful hand of the living does not desert the hand of
    the dying,
The twitching lips press lightly on the forehead of the
    dying,
The breath ceases, and the pulse of the heart ceases,
The corpse stretches on the bed, and the living look upon
    it,
It is palpable as the living are palpable.

The living look upon the corpse with their eyesight,
But without eyesight lingers a different living, and looks
    curiously on the corpse.

3.

To think that the rivers will flow, and the snow fall, and
    the fruits ripen, and act upon others as upon us now—
    yet not act upon us!
To think of all these wonders of city and country, and
    others taking great interest in them—and we taking—
    no interest in them!

To think how eager we are in building our houses!
To think others shall be just as eager, and we quite
    indifferent!
I see one building the house that serves him a few years,
    or seventy or eighty years at most,
I see one building the house that serves him longer than
    that.

Slow-moving and black lines creep over the whole earth—
 they never cease— they are the burial lines;
He that was President was buried, and he that is now
 President shall surely be buried.

4.

Gold dash of waves at the ferry-wharf—posh and ice
 in the river, half- frozen mud in the streets, a grey
 discouraged sky overhead, the short last daylight of
 Twelfth-month,
A hearse and stages—other vehicles give place—the
 funeral of an old Broadway stage-driver, the cortege
 mostly drivers.

Steady the trot to the cemetery, duly rattles the death-bell,
 the gate is passed, the new-dug grave is halted at, the
 living alight, the hearse uncloses,
The coffin is passed out, lowered, and settled, the whip is
 laid on the coffin, the earth is swiftly shovelled in,
The mound above is flattened with the spades—silence,
A minute, no one moves or speaks—it is done,
He is decently put away—is there anything more?
He was a good fellow, free-mouthed, quick-tempered,
 not bad-looking, able to take his own part, witty,
 sensitive to a slight, ready with life or death for a
 friend, fond of women, gambled, ate hearty, drank
 hearty, had known what it was to be flush, grew low-
 spirited toward the last, sickened, was helped by a
 contribution, died, aged forty- one years—and that
 was his funeral.

Thumb extended, finger uplifted, apron, cape, gloves,
 strap, wet-weather clothes, whip carefully chosen,
 boss, spotter, starter, hostler, somebody loafing on

you, you loafing on somebody, headway, man before
and man behind, good day's work, bad day's work,
pet stock, mean stock, first out, last out, turning-in at
night;
To think that these are so much and so nigh to other
drivers—and he there takes no interest in them!

5.

The markets, the government, the working-man's wages—
to think what account they are through our nights
and days!
To think that other working-men will make just as great
account of them— yet we make little or no account!
The vulgar and the refined—what you call sin, and what
you call goodness— to think how wide a difference!
To think the difference will still continue to others, yet we
lie beyond the difference.

To think how much pleasure there is!
Have you pleasure from looking at the sky? have you
pleasure from poems?
Do you enjoy yourself in the city? or engaged in business?
or planning a nomination and election? or with your
wife and family?
Or with your mother and sisters? or in womanly
housework? or the beautiful maternal cares?
These also flow onward to others—you and I fly onward,
But in due time you and I shall take less interest in them.

Your farm, profits, crops,—to think how engrossed you
are! To think there will still be farms, profits, crops—
yet for you, of what avail?

6.

What will be will be well—for what is is well;
To take interest is well, and not to take interest shall be
    well.

The sky continues beautiful,
The pleasure of men with women shall never be sated, nor
    the pleasure of women with men, nor the pleasure
    from poems;
The domestic joys, the daily housework or business, the
    building of houses—these are not phantasms—they
    have weight, form, location;
Farms, profits, crops, markets, wages, government, are
    none of them phantasms;
The difference between sin and goodness is no delusion,
The earth is not an echo—man and his life, and all the
    things of his life, are well-considered.

You are not thrown to the winds—you gather certainly
    and safely around yourself;
Yourself! Yourself! Yourself, for ever and ever!

7.

It is not to diffuse you that you were born of your mother
    and father—it is to identify you;
It is not that you should be undecided, but that you should
    be decided;
Something long preparing and formless is arrived and
    formed in you,
You are henceforth secure, whatever comes or goes.

The threads that were spun are gathered, the weft crosses
    the warp, the pattern is systematic.

The preparations have every one been justified,
The orchestra have sufficiently tuned their instruments—
   the baton has given the signal.

The guest that was coming—he waited long, for reasons—
   he is now housed;
He is one of those who are beautiful and happy—he is one
   of those that to look upon and be with is enough.

The law of the past cannot be eluded,
The law of the present and future cannot be eluded,
The law of the living cannot be eluded—it is eternal;
The law of promotion and transformation cannot be
   eluded,
The law of heroes and good-doers cannot be eluded,
The law of drunkards, informers, mean persons—not one
   iota thereof can be eluded.

8.

Slow-moving and black lines go ceaselessly over the earth,
Northerner goes carried, and Southerner goes carried,
      and they on the Atlantic side, and they on the Pacific,
      and they between, and all through the Mississippi
      country, and all over the earth.

The great masters and kosmos are well as they go—the
   heroes and good-doers are well,
The known leaders and inventors, and the rich owners
   and pious and distinguished, may be well,
But there is more account than that—there is strict
   account of all.

The interminable hordes of the ignorant and wicked are
    not nothing,
The barbarians of Africa and Asia are not nothing,
The common people of Europe are not nothing—the
    American aborigines are not nothing,
The infected in the immigrant hospital are not nothing—
    the murderer or mean person is not nothing,
The perpetual successions of shallow people are not
    nothing as they go,
The lowest prostitute is not nothing—the mocker of
    religion is not nothing as he goes.

9.

I shall go with the rest—we have satisfaction,
I have dreamed that we are not to be changed so much,
    nor the law of us changed,
I have dreamed that heroes and good-doers shall be under
    the present and past law,
And that murderers, drunkards, liars, shall be under the
    present and past law,
For I have dreamed that the law they are under now is
    enough.

And I have dreamed that the satisfaction is not so much
    changed, and that there is no life without satisfaction;
What is the earth? what are Body and Soul without
    satisfaction?

I shall go with the rest,
We cannot be stopped at a given point—that is no
    satisfaction,
To show us a good thing, or a few good things, for a space
    of time—that is no satisfaction,

We must have the indestructible breed of the best,
    regardless of time.

If otherwise, all these things came but to ashes of dung,
If maggots and rats ended us, then alarum! for we are
    betrayed!
Then indeed suspicion of death.

Do you suspect death? If I were to suspect death, I should
    die now:
Do you think I could walk pleasantly and well-suited
    toward annihilation?

10.

Pleasantly and well-suited I walk:
Whither I walk I cannot define, but I know it is good;
The whole universe indicates that it is good,
The past and the present indicate that it is good.

How beautiful and perfect are the animals! How perfect is
    my Soul!
How perfect the earth, and the minutest thing upon it!
What is called good is perfect, and what is called bad is
    just as perfect,
The vegetables and minerals are all perfect, and the
    imponderable fluids are perfect;
Slowly and surely they have passed on to this, and slowly
    and surely they yet pass on.

My Soul! if I realise you, I have satisfaction;
Animals and vegetables! if I realise you, I have
    satisfaction;
Laws of the earth and air! if I realise you, I have
    satisfaction.

I cannot define my satisfaction, yet it is so;
I cannot define my life, yet it is so.

11.

It comes to me now!
I swear I think now that everything without exception has
an eternal soul!
The trees have, rooted in the ground! the weeds of the sea
have! the animals!

I swear I think there is nothing but immortality!
That the exquisite scheme is for it, and the nebulous float
is for it, and the cohering is for it;
And all preparation is for it! and identity is for it! and life
and death are altogether for it!

THIS COMPOST.

1.

Something startles me where I thought I was safest;
I withdraw from the still woods I loved;
I will not go now on the pastures to walk;
I will not strip the clothes from my body to meet my lover
the sea;
I will not touch my flesh to the earth, as to other flesh, to
renew me.

2.

O how can the ground not sicken?
How can you be alive, you growths of spring?
How can you furnish health, you blood of herbs, roots,
orchards, grain?
Are they not continually putting distempered corpses in
you?
Is not every continent worked over and over with sour
dead?

Where have you disposed of their carcasses?
Those drunkards and gluttons of so many generations;
Where have you drawn off all the foul liquid and meat?
I do not see any of it upon you to-day—or perhaps I am
deceived;
I will run a furrow with my plough—I will press my spade
through the sod, and turn it up underneath;
I am sure I shall expose some of the foul meat.

3.

Behold this compost! behold it well!
Perhaps every mite has once formed part of a sick
    person—Yet behold!
The grass covers the prairies,
The bean bursts noiselessly through the mould in the
    garden,
The delicate spear of the onion pierces upward,
The apple-buds cluster together on the apple branches,
The resurrection of the wheat appears with pale visage out
    of its graves,
The tinge awakes over the willow-tree and the mulberry-
    tree,
The he-birds carol mornings and evenings, while the she-
    birds sit on their nests,
The young of poultry break through the hatched eggs,
The new-born of animals appear—the calf is dropped
    from the cow, the colt from the mare,
Out of its little hill faithfully rise the potato's dark-green
    leaves,
Out of its hill rises the yellow maize-stalk;
The summer growth is innocent and disdainful above all
    those strata of sour dead.

What chemistry!
That the winds are really not infectious,
That this is no cheat, this transparent green-wash of the
    sea, which is so amorous after me;
That it is safe to allow it to lick my naked body all over
    with its tongues,
That it will not endanger me with the fevers that have
    deposited themselves in it,
That all is clean for ever and for ever,
That the cool drink from the well tastes so good,

That blackberries are so flavorous and juicy,
That the fruits of the apple-orchard, and of the orange-
   orchard—that melons, grapes, peaches, plums, will
   none of them poison me,
That when I recline on the grass I do not catch any
   disease,
Though probably every sphere of grass rises out of what
   was once a catching disease.

4.

Now I am terrified at the Earth! it is that calm and
   patient,
It grows such sweet things out of such corruptions,
It turns harmless and stainless on its axis, with such
   endless successions of diseased corpses,
It distils such exquisite winds out of such infused fetor,
It renews with such unwitting looks its prodigal, annual,
   sumptuous crops,
It gives such divine materials to men, and accepts such
   leavings from them at last.

DESPAIRING CRIES.

1.

Despairing cries float ceaselessly toward me, day and
    night,
The sad voice of Death—the call of my nearest lover,
    putting forth, alarmed, uncertain,
*"The Sea I am quickly to sail: come tell me, Come tell me
    where I am speeding—tell me my destination."*

2.

I understand your anguish, but I cannot help you;
I approach, hear, behold—the sad mouth, the look out of
    the eyes, your mute inquiry,
"Whither I go from the bed I recline on, come tell me."
Old age, alarmed, uncertain—A young woman's voice,
    appealing to me for comfort;
A young man's voice, *"Shall I not escape?"*

THE CITY DEAD-HOUSE

By the City Dead-House, by the gate,
As idly sauntering, wending my way from the clangour,
I curious pause—for lo! an outcast form, a poor dead
    prostitute brought;

Her corpse they deposit unclaimed, it lies on the damp
    brick pavement.
The divine woman, her body—I see the body—I look on
    it alone,
That house once full of passion and beauty—all else I
    notice not;
Nor stillness so cold, nor running water from faucet, nor
    odours morbific impress me;
But the house alone—that wondrous house—that delicate
    fair house—that ruin!
That immortal house, more than all the rows of dwellings
    ever built,
Or white-domed Capitol itself, with majestic figure
    surmounted—or all the old high-spired cathedrals,
That little house alone, more than them all—poor,
    desperate house!
Fair, fearful wreck! tenement of a Soul! itself a Soul!
Unclaimed, avoided house! take one breath from my
    tremulous lips;

Take one tear, dropped aside as I go, for thought of you,
Dead house of love! house of madness and sin, crumbled!
    crushed!

House of life—erewhile talking and laughing—but ah,
    poor house! dead even then;
Months, years, an echoing, garnished house-but dead,
    dead, dead!

TO ONE SHORTLY TO DIE.

1.

From all the rest I single out you, having a message for
    you:
You are to die—Let others tell you what they please, I
    cannot prevaricate,
I am exact and merciless, but I love you—There is no
    escape for you.

2.

Softly I lay my right hand upon you—you just feel it;
I do not argue—I bend my head close, and half envelop it,
I sit quietly by—I remain faithful,
I am more than nurse, more than parent or neighbour,
I absolve you from all except yourself, spiritual, bodily—
    that is eternal,—
The corpse you will leave will be but excrementitious.

The sun bursts through in unlooked-for directions!
Strong thoughts fill you, and confidence—you smile!
You forget you are sick, as I forget you are sick,
You do not see the medicines—you do not mind the
    weeping friends—I am with you,
I exclude others from you—there is nothing to be
    commiserated,
I do not commiserate—I congratulate you.

UNNAMED LANDS.

1.

Nations, ten thousand years before these States, and many
    times ten thousand years before these States;
Garnered clusters of ages, that men and women like us
    grew up and travelled their course, and passed on;
What vast-built cities—what orderly republics—what
    pastoral tribes and nomads;
What histories, rulers, heroes, perhaps transcending all
    others;
What laws, customs, wealth, arts, traditions;
What sort of marriage—what costumes—what physiology
    and phrenology;
What of liberty and slavery among them—what they
    thought of death and the soul;
Who were witty and wise—who beautiful and poetic—
    who brutish and undeveloped;
Not a mark, not a record remains,—And yet all remains.

2.

O I know that those men and women were not for
    nothing, any more than we are for nothing;
I know that they belong to the scheme of the world every
    bit as much as we now belong to it, and as all will
    henceforth belong to it.

Afar they stand—yet near to me they stand,
Some with oval countenances, learned and calm,

Some naked and savage—Some like huge collections of
   insects,
Some in tents—herdsmen, patriarchs, tribes, horsemen,
Some prowling through woods—Some living peaceably
   on farms, labouring, reaping, filling barns,
Some traversing paved avenues, amid temples, palaces,
   factories, libraries, shows, courts, theatres, wonderful
   monuments.

Are those billions of men really gone?
Are those women of the old experience of the earth gone?
Do their lives, cities, arts, rest only with us?
Did they achieve nothing for good, for themselves?

3.

I believe, of all those billions of men and women that
   filled the unnamed lands, every one exists this hour,
   here or elsewhere, invisible to us, in exact proportion
   to what he or she grew from in life, and out of what he
   or she did, felt, became, loved, sinned, in life.

I believe that was not the end of those nations, or any
   person of them, any more than this shall be the end of
   my nation, or of me;
Of their languages, governments, marriage, literature,
   products, games, wars, manners, crimes, prisons,
   slaves, heroes, poets, I suspect their results curiously
   await in the yet unseen world—counterparts of what
   accrued to them in the seen world;
I suspect I shall meet them there,
I suspect I shall there find each old particular of those
   unnamed lands.

SIMILITUDE.

1.

On the beach at night alone,
As the old Mother sways her to and fro, singing her
   savage and husky song,
As I watch the bright stars shining—I think a thought of
   the clef of the universes, and of the future.

2.

A VAST SIMILITUDE interlocks all,
All spheres, grown, ungrown, small, large, suns, moons,
   planets, comets, asteroids,
All the substances of the same, and all that is spiritual
   upon the same,
All distances of place, however wide,
All distances of time—all inanimate forms,
All Souls—all living bodies, though they be ever so
   different, or in different worlds,
All gaseous, watery, vegetable, mineral processes—the
   fishes, the brutes,
All men and women—me also;
All nations, colours, barbarisms, civilisations, languages;
All identities that have existed, or may exist, on this globe,
   or any globe;
All lives and deaths—all of the past, present, future;
This vast similitude spans them, and always has spanned,
   and shall for ever span them, and compactly hold
   them.

THE SQUARE DEIFIC.

God.

Chanting the Square Deific, out of the One advancing, out
    of the sides;
Out of the old and new—out of the square entirely divine,
Solid, four-sided, (all the sides needed)—From this side
    JEHOVAH am I,
Old Brahm I, and I Saturnius am;
Not Time affects me—I am Time, modern as any;
Unpersuadable, relentless, executing righteous judgments;
As the Earth, the Father, the brown old Kronos, with laws,
Aged beyond computation—yet ever new—ever with
    those mighty laws rolling,
Relentless, I forgive no man—whoever sins dies—I will
    have that man's life;
Therefore let none expect mercy—Have the seasons,
    gravitation, the appointed days, mercy?—No more
    have I;
But as the seasons, and gravitation—and as all the
    appointed days, that forgive not,
I dispense from this side judgments inexorable, without
    the least remorse.

SAVIOUR.

Consolator most mild, the promised one advancing,
With gentle hand extended, the mightier God am I,
Foretold by prophets and poets, in their most wrapt
    prophecies and poems;
From this side, lo! the Lord CHRIST gazes—lo! Hermes
    I—lo! mine is Hercules' face;
All sorrow, labour, suffering, I, tallying it, absorb in
    myself;
Many times have I been rejected, taunted, put in prison,
    and crucified—and many times shall be again;
All the world have I given up for my dear brothers' and
    sisters' sake—for the soul's sake;
Wending my way through the homes of men, rich or poor,
    with the kiss of affection;
For I am affection—I am the cheer-bringing God, with
    hope, and all- enclosing charity;
Conqueror yet—for before me all the armies and soldiers
    of the earth shall yet bow—and all the weapons of war
    become impotent:
With indulgent words, as to children—with fresh and
    sane words, mine only;
Young and strong I pass, knowing well I am destined
    myself to an early death:
But my Charity has no death—my Wisdom dies not,
    neither early nor late,
And my sweet Love, bequeathed here and elsewhere,
    never dies.

SATAN.

Aloof, dissatisfied, plotting revolt,
Comrade of criminals, brother of slaves,
Crafty, despised, a drudge, ignorant,
With sudra face and worn brow—black, but in the depths
    of my heart proud as any;
Lifted, now and always, against whoever, scorning,
    assumes to rule me;
Morose, full of guile, full of reminiscences, brooding,
    with many wiles,
Though it was thought I was baffled and dispelled, and
    my wiles done—but that will never be;
Defiant I SATAN still live—still utter words—in new
    lands duly appearing, and old ones also;
Permanent here, from my side, warlike, equal with any,
    real as any,
Nor time, nor change, shall ever change me or my words.

THE SPIRIT.

Santa SPIRITA,[1] breather, life,
Beyond the light, lighter than light,
Beyond the flames of hell—joyous, leaping easily above
    hell;
Beyond Paradise—perfumed solely with mine own
    perfume;
Including all life on earth—touching, including God—
    including Saviour and Satan;
Ethereal, pervading all—for, without me, what were all?
    what were God?
Essence of forms—life of the real identities, permanent,
    positive, namely the unseen,
Life of the great round world, the sun and stars, and of
    man—I, the General Soul,
Here the Square finishing, the solid, I the most solid,
Breathe my breath also through these little songs.

FOOTNOTES:

1. *The reader will share my wish that Whitman had written*
   sanctus spiritus, which is right, instead of santa spirita, which is
   methodically wrong.

SONGS OF PARTING.

SINGERS AND POETS.

1.

The indications and tally of time;
Perfect sanity shows the master among philosophs;
Time, always without flaw, indicates itself in parts;
What always indicates the poet is the crowd of the
     pleasant company of singers, and their words;
The words of the singers are the hours or minutes of the
     light or dark—but the words of the maker of poems
     are the general light and dark;
The maker of poems settles justice, reality, immortality,
His insight and power encircle things and the human
     race,
He is the glory and extract, thus far, of things and of the
     human race.

2.

The singers do not beget—only the POET begets;
The singers are welcomed, understood, appear often
     enough—but rare has the day been, likewise the spot,
     of the birth of the maker of poems;
Not every century, or every five centuries, has contained
     such a day, for all its names.
The singers of successive hours of centuries may have
     ostensible names, but the name of each of them is one
     of the singers;

The name of each is eye-singer, ear-singer, head-singer,
    sweet-singer, echo-singer, parlour-singer, love-singer,
    or something else.

3.

All this time, and at all times, wait the words of poems;
The greatness of sons is the exuding of the greatness of
    mothers and fathers;
The words of poems are the tuft and final applause of
    science.

Divine instinct, breadth of vision, the law of reason,
    health, rudeness of body, withdrawnness, gaiety,
    sun-tan, air-sweetness—such are some of the words of
    poems.

4.

The sailor and traveller underlie the maker of poems,
 The builder, geometer, chemist, anatomist, phrenologist,
    artist—all these underlie the maker of poems.

5.

The words of the true poems give you more than poems,
They give you, to form for yourself, poems, religions,
    politics, war, peace, behaviour, histories, essays,
    romances, and everything else,
They balance ranks, colours, races, creeds, and the sexes,
They do not seek beauty—they are sought,
For ever touching them, or close upon them, follows
    beauty, longing, fain, love-sick.

They prepare for death—yet are they not the finish, but
    rather the outset,
They bring none to his or her terminus, or to be content
    and full;
Whom they take, they take into space, to behold the birth
    of stars, to learn one of the meanings,
To launch off with absolute faith—to sweep through the
    ceaseless rings, and never be quiet again.

TO A HISTORIAN.

You who celebrate bygones:
Who have explored the outward, the surfaces of the
    races—the life that has exhibited itself;
Who have treated of man as the creature of politics,
    aggregates, rulers, and priests.
I, habitué of the Alleghanies, treating man as he is in
    himself, in his own rights,
Pressing the pulse of the life that has seldom exhibited
    itself, the great pride of man in himself;
Chanter of Personality, outlining what is yet to be;
I project the history of the future.

FIT AUDIENCE.

1.

Whoever you are, holding me now in hand,
Without one thing, all will be useless:
I give you fair warning, before you attempt me further,
I am not what you supposed, but far different.

2.

Who is he that would become my follower?
Who would sign himself a candidate for my affections?

The way is suspicious—the result uncertain, perhaps
    destructive;
You would have to give up all else—I alone would expect
    to be your God, sole and exclusive;
Your novitiate would even then be long and exhausting,
The whole past theory of your life, and all conformity to
    the lives around you, would have to be abandoned;
Therefore release me now, before troubling yourself any
    further—Let go your hand from my shoulders,
Put me down, and depart on your way.

Or else, by stealth, in some wood, for trial,
Or back of a rock, in the open air,
(For in any roofed room of a house I emerge not—nor in
    company,
And in libraries I lie as one dumb, a gawk, or unborn, or
    dead,)

But just possibly with you on a high hill—first watching
    lest any person, for miles around, approach
    unawares—
Or possibly with you sailing at sea, or on the beach of the
    sea, or some quiet island,
Here to put your lips upon mine I permit you,
With the comrade's long-dwelling kiss, or the new
    husband's kiss,
For I am the new husband, and I am the comrade.

Or, if you will, thrusting me beneath your clothing,
Where I may feel the throbs of your heart, or rest upon
    your hip,
Carry me when you go forth over land or sea;
For thus, merely touching you, is enough—is best,
And thus, touching you, would I silently sleep, and be
    carried eternally.

3.

But these leaves conning, you con at peril,
For these leaves, and me, you will not understand,
They will elude you at first, and still more afterward—I
    will certainly elude you,
Even while you should think you had unquestionably
    caught me, behold!
Already you see I have escaped from you.

For it is not for what I have put into it that I have written
    this book,
Nor is it by reading it you will acquire it,
Nor do those know me best who admire me, and
    vauntingly praise me,
Nor will the candidates for my love (unless at most a very
    few) prove victorious,

Nor will my poems do good only—they will do just as
 much evil, perhaps more;
For all is useless without that which you may guess at
 many times and not hit—that which I hinted at;
Therefore release me, and depart on your way.

SINGING IN SPRING.

———————

These I, singing in spring, collect for lovers:
For who but I should understand lovers, and all their
    sorrow and joy?
And who but I should be the poet of comrades?
Collecting, I traverse the garden, the world—but soon I
    pass the gates,
Now along the pond-side—now wading in a little, fearing
    not the wet,
Now by the post-and-rail fences, where the old
    stones thrown there, picked from the fields, have
    accumulated,
Wild flowers and vines and weeds come up through the
    stones, and partly cover them—Beyond these I pass,
Far, far in the forest, before I think where I go,
Solitary, smelling the earthy smell, stopping now and then
    in the silence;
Alone, I had thought—yet soon a silent troop gathers
    around me;
Some walk by my side, and some behind, and some
    embrace my arms or neck,
They, the spirits of friends, dead or alive—thicker they
    come, a great crowd, and I in the middle,
Collecting, dispensing, singing in spring, there I wander
    with them,
Plucking something for tokens—tossing toward whoever
    is near me.
Here lilac, with a branch of pine,
Here, out of my pocket, some moss which I pulled off a
    live-oak in Florida, as it hung trailing down,

Here some pinks and laurel leaves, and a handful of sage,
And here what I now draw from the water, wading in the
    pond-side,
(O here I last saw him that tenderly loves me—and
    returns again, never to separate from me,
And this, O this shall henceforth be the token of
    comrades—this Calamus- root[1] shall,
Interchange it, youths, with each other! Let none render it
    back!)
And twigs of maple, and a bunch of wild orange, and
    chestnut,
And stems of currants, and plum-blows, and the aromatic
    cedar,
These I, compassed around by a thick cloud of spirits,
Wandering, point to, or touch as I pass, or throw them
    loosely from me,
Indicating to each one what he shall have—giving
    something to each.
But what I drew from the water by the pond-side, that I
    reserve;
I will give of it—but only to them that love as I myself am
    capable of loving.

FOOTNOTES:

1. *I am favoured with the following indication, from Mr Whitman
himself, of the relation in which this word Calamus is to be
understood:—"Calamus is the very large and aromatic grass
or rush growing about water-ponds in the valleys—spears
about three feet high; often called Sweet Flag; grows all over the
Northern and Middle States. The recherché or ethereal sense of
the term, as used in my book, arises probably from the actual
Calamus presenting the biggest and hardiest kind of spears of
grass, and their fresh, aquatic, pungent bouquet."*

LOVE OF COMRADES.

1.

Come, I will make the continent indissoluble;
I will make the most splendid race the sun ever yet shone
    upon!
I will make divine magnetic lands,
        With the love of comrades,
            With the life-long love of comrades.

2.

I will plant companionship thick as trees along all the
    rivers of America, and along the shores of the great
    lakes, and all over the prairies;
I will make inseparable cities, with their arms about each
    other's necks;
        By the love of comrades,
            By the manly love of comrades.

3.

For you these, from me, O Democracy, to serve you, *ma
    femme*!
For you! for you, I am trilling these songs,
        In the love of comrades,
            In the high-towering love of comrades.

PULSE OF MY LIFE.

Not heaving from my ribbed breast only;
Not in sighs at night, in rage, dissatisfied with myself;
Not in those long-drawn, ill-suppressed sighs;
Not in many an oath and promise broken;
Not in my wilful and savage soul's volition;
Not in the subtle nourishment of the air;
Not in this beating and pounding at my temples and
    wrists;
Not in the curious systole and diastole within, which will
    one day cease;
Not in many a hungry wish, told to the skies only;
Not in cries, laughter, defiances, thrown from me when
    alone, far in the wilds;
Not in husky pantings through clenched teeth;
Not in sounded and resounded words—chattering words,
    echoes, dead words;
Not in the murmurs of my dreams while I sleep,
Nor the other murmurs of these incredible dreams of
    every day;
Nor in the limbs and senses of my body, that take you and
    dismiss you continually—Not there;
Not in any or all of them, O Adhesiveness! O pulse of my
    life!
Need I that you exist and show yourself, any more than in
    these songs.

AUXILIARIES.

WHAT place is besieged, and vainly tries to raise the
    siege?
Lo! I send to that place a commander, swift, brave,
    immortal;
And with him horse and foot, and parks of artillery,
And artillerymen, the deadliest that ever fired gun.

REALITIES.

1.

As I walk, solitary, unattended,
Around me I hear that *éclat* of the world—politics,
    produce,
The announcements of recognised things—science,
The approved growth of cities, and the spread of
    inventions.
I see the ships, (they will last a few years,)
The vast factories, with their foremen and workmen,
And hear the endorsement of all, and do not object to it.

2.

But I too announce solid things;
Science, ships, politics, cities, factories, are not nothing—
    they serve,
They stand for realities—all is as it should be.

3.

Then my realities;
What else is so real as mine?
Libertad, and the divine Average-Freedom to every slave
    on the face of the earth,
The rapt promises and *luminé*[1] of seers—the spiritual
    world—these centuries-lasting songs,
And our visions, the visions of poets, the most solid
    announcements of any.

For we support all,
After the rest is done and gone, we remain,
There is no final reliance but upon us;
Democracy rests finally upon us, (I, my brethren, begin
    it,)
And our visions sweep through eternity.

FOOTNOTES:

1. *I suppose Whitman gets this odd word luminé, by a process of his own, out of illuminati, and intends it to stand for what would be called clairvoyance, intuition.*

NEARING DEPARTURE.

1.

As nearing departure,
As the time draws nigh, glooming, a cloud,
A dread beyond, of I know not what, darkens me.

2.

I shall *go* forth,
I shall traverse the States—but I cannot tell whither or
    how long;
Perhaps soon, some day or night while I am singing, my
    voice will suddenly cease.

3.

O book and chant! must all then amount to but this?
Must we barely arrive at this beginning of me?…
And yet it is enough, O soul!
O soul! we have positively appeared—that is enough.

POETS TO COME.

1.

Poets to come!
Not to-day is to justify me, and Democracy, and what we
    are for;
But you, a new brood, native, athletic, continental, greater
    than before known,
You must justify me.

2.

I but write one or two indicative words for the future,
I but advance a moment, only to wheel and hurry back in
    the darkness.

I am a man who, sauntering along, without fully stopping,
    turns a casual look upon you, and then averts his face,
Leaving it to you to prove and define it,
Expecting the main things from you.

CENTURIES HENCE.

Full of life now, compact, visible,
I, forty years old the eighty-third year of the States,
To one a century hence, or any number of centuries
    hence,
To you, yet unborn, these seeking you.

When you read these, I, that was visible, am become
    invisible;
Now it is you, compact, visible, realising my poems,
    seeking me;
Fancying how happy you were, if I could be with you, and
    become your loving comrade;
Be it as if I were with you. Be not too certain but I am now
    with you.

SO LONG!

1.

To conclude—I announce what comes after me;
I announce mightier offspring, orators, days, and then
  depart,

I remember I said, before my leaves sprang at all,
I would raise my voice jocund and strong, with reference
  to consummations.

When America does what was promised,
When there are plentiful athletic bards, inland and sea-
  board,
When through these States walk a hundred millions of
  superb persons,
When the rest part away for superb persons, and
  contribute to them,
When breeds of the most perfect mothers denote
  America,
Then to me my due fruition.

I have pressed through in my own right,
I have offered my style to every one—I have journeyed
  with confident step.
While my pleasure is yet at the full, I whisper, *So long!*
And take the young woman's hand, and the young man's
  hand for the last time.

2.

I announce natural persons to arise,
I announce justice triumphant,
I announce uncompromising liberty and equality,
I announce the justification of candour, and the
   justification of pride.

I announce that the identity of these States is a single
   identity only,
I announce the Union, out of all its struggles and wars,
   more and more compact,
I announce splendours and majesties to make all the
   previous politics of the earth insignificant.

I announce a man or woman coming—perhaps you are
   the one (*So long!*)
I announce the great individual, fluid as Nature, chaste,
   affectionate, compassionate, fully armed.

I announce a life that shall be copious, vehement,
   spiritual, bold,
And I announce an old age that shall lightly and joyfully
   meet its translation.

3.

O thicker and faster! (*So long!*)
O crowding too close upon me;
I foresee too much—it means more than I thought,
It appears to me I am dying.

Hasten throat, and sound your last!
Salute me—salute the days once more. Peal the old cry
   once more.

Screaming electric, the atmosphere using,
At random glancing, each as I notice absorbing,
Swiftly on, but a little while alighting,
Curious enveloped messages delivering,

Sparkles hot, seed ethereal, down in the dirt dropping,
Myself unknowing, my commission obeying, to question
    it never daring,
To ages, and ages yet, the growth of the seed leaving,
To troops out of me rising—they the tasks I have set
    promulging,
To women certain whispers of myself bequeathing—their
    affection me more clearly explaining,
To young men my problems offering—no dallier I—I the
    muscle of their brains trying,
So I pass—a little time vocal, visible, contrary,
Afterward, a melodious echo, passionately bent for—
    death making me really undying,—
The best of me then when no longer visible—for toward
    that I have been incessantly preparing.

What is there more, that I lag and pause, and crouch
    extended with unshut mouth?
Is there a single final farewell?

4.

My songs cease—I abandon them,
From behind the screen where I hid, I advance personally,
    solely to you.

Camerado! This is no book;
Who touches this touches a man.
(Is it night? Are we here alone?)

It is I you hold, and who holds you,
I spring from the pages into your arms—decease calls me
    forth.

O how your fingers drowse me!
Your breath falls around me like dew—your pulse lulls
    the tympans of my ears,
I feel immerged from head to foot,
Delicious—enough.

Enough, O deed impromptu and secret!
Enough, O gliding present! Enough, O summed-up past!

5.

Dear friend, whoever you are, here, take this kiss,
I give it especially to you—Do not forget me,
I feel like one who has done his work—I progress on,—
    (long enough have I dallied with Life,)
The unknown sphere, more real than I dreamed, more
    direct, awakening rays about me—*So long*!
Remember my words—I love you—I depart from
    materials,
I am as one disembodied, triumphant, dead.

POSTSCRIPT.

While this Selection was passing through the press, it has been my privilege to receive two letters from Mr. Whitman, besides another communicated to me through a friend. I find my experience to be the same as that of some previous writers: that, if one admires Whitman in reading his books, one loves him on coming into any personal relation with him—even the comparatively distant relation of letter-writing.

The more I have to thank the poet for the substance and tone of his letters, and some particular expressions in them, the more does it become incumbent upon me to guard against any misapprehension. He has had nothing whatever to do with this Selection, as to either prompting, guiding, or even ratifying it: except only that he did not prohibit my making two or three verbal omissions in the *Prose Preface to the Leaves of Grass*, and he has supplied his own title, *President Lincoln's Funeral Hymn*, to a poem which, in my Prefatory Notice, is named (by myself) *Nocturn for the Death of Lincoln*. All admirers of his poetry will rejoice to learn that there is no longer any doubt of his adding to his next edition "a brief cluster of pieces born of thoughts on the deep themes of Death and Immortality." A new American edition will be dear to many: a complete English edition ought to be an early demand of English poetic readers, and would be the right and crowning result of the present Selection.

W. M. R.
868.

370

www.ingramcontent.com/pod-product-compliance
Lightning Source LLC
Chambersburg PA
CBHW020419030726
47495CB00006B/1584